Celtic Fire

Evangelism in the Wisdom and Power of the Spirit

Celtic Fire

Evangelism in the Wisdom and Power of the Spirit

William J. Abraham

HIGHLAND
LOCH PRESS
Dallas, TX

To the

Rev. Dinu Petrache

A True Methodist Evangelist

Contents

Acknowledgements

I am delighted to acknowledge the help of Anthony Cunningham for extended assistance in bringing this book to press. His gimlet eye for detail is a godsend.

I am also delighted to acknowledge the permission of a wonderful photographer, Melissa Autumn Collins, to use her image of the Celtic Cross from Devenish Island, in my beloved Country Fermanagh, for the front and back cover.

Preface

This book represents my last will and testament in evangelism. It is addressed initially and directly to Methodists across the world; indirectly it is also a word to the whole Church. What has happened in Methodism in the United States is, in fact, a salutary lesson for all Christians. While the focus of this book is Methodism, its content has universal significance for all Christians.

This material represents the Denman Lectures which I was privileged to give in 2009 in Nashville, Tennessee. I am extremely grateful to The Foundation for Evangelism for the invitation to give these lectures and to the audience who heard them live. Aside from cosmetic changes, they remain pretty much the same as delivered.

I argue here that it was no accident that Methodism made an extraordinary contribution to evangelism across its short history.[1] To use the language of Charles Wesley, Methodism in its evangelism did unite the pair so long disjoin'd, knowledge and vital piety. In time, however, these two split apart and took on careers of their own. The future in evangelism lies with all those inside and outside of Methodism who can find a way to put them back together again. It is an open question whether United Methodism as expressed in the United States of America can do this. The signs at the moment are bleak. Its leaders – women and men of fierce sincerity and integrity – are not currently prepared to make the radical changes that are needed to get on course for the future. Local churches can, of course, ignore a misleading and dysfunctional leadership; many are doing exactly that. However, it is a platitude that any denomination cannot make deep progress if its leaders have lost the plot in evangelism or are preoccupied with other things. The issue is not one of personal faith or integrity; it is a mat-

---

[1] Those seeking a comprehensive account of Methodism should consult William J. Abraham and James E. Kirby, eds., *The Oxford Handbook of Methodist Studies* (Oxford: Oxford University Press, 2009).

ter of corporate vision, will, and action. All this may change, but only time will tell. Happily, there are others in the Methodist and Wesleyan family scattered across the world that are much more likely to heed the word delivered here.

Evangelism, however, is much too important a ministry of the Church to be left to Methodists. Hence, I hope that those outside its walls will read this book to their profit. The challenges that Methodism faced and have failed to address in the United States over the last century are not peculiar to Methodism. They are pivotal to the churches of the West; and they will become in time inescapable to churches outside the West. Thus I dare to offer this to the whole Church of Jesus Christ, the one and only Savior of the world.

1. Holy Smoke

Introduction: the Aim of this Work

It is a singular honor for me to be asked to deliver the Denman Lectures on evangelism. I never knew Harry Denman, but I have read about him, and I have heard a host of stories about him over the last twenty years in Texas. Clearly he is one of the great saints and heroes of Methodism; more specifically he is one of the great saints and heroes of evangelism in our tradition. So it is an honor to celebrate his life and work by taking time to think about the theory and practice of evangelism in our day. It is also a great honor because of the long line of distinguished lecturers who have delivered the Denman Lectures. No name stands out more clearly in this list than that of Professor Albert Cook Outler, one of the truly extraordinary figures in our tradition, who delivered the Denman Lectures in 1971. When I first came to Perkins School of Theology, Outler was still in the area, so I was able to meet him there on various occasions. Little did I know then that one day I would have the honor of holding the Outler Chair of Wesley Studies. So I have additional reasons for celebration and gratitude.

When Outler delivered his lectures I was in Wilmore, Kentucky in the middle of my first year at Asbury Theological Seminary. This was nearly forty years ago. Having given a lot of time and energy to evangelism over these last thirty years, I welcome the opportunity to share my own present reflections on the theory and practice of evangelism. This year also coincides with the twentieth anniversary of the publication of my book, *The Logic of Evangelism*.[2] So this may be my lucky year: some folk may actually be interested in what I have to say after all these years.

My aim in these lectures is simple. I want to review the legacy that has been bequeathed to us in evangelism in Methodism. I shall begin

---

[2] William J. Abraham, *The Logic of Evangelism* (Grand Rapids, Mich: W.B. Eerdmans, 1989).

by mapping the most influential vision of evangelism that has informed our work over the last generation. I shall then contrast this with a very different vision of the theory and practice of evangelism developed by a fascinating Methodist intellectual and evangelist outside of United Methodism. In my third lecture I shall go back behind these options and explore the significance of evangelism as read through the lens of an influential evangelist from the nineteenth century. Given the time constraints there will be no effort to offer a comprehensive overview of all the options that are currently in the air. We are in fact blessed now to have a much better canon of literature on evangelism than we did when I wrote *The Logic of Evangelism*. My method will be one of staying focused and going deep.

The Significance of Albert Cook Outler

My mention of Albert Outler was not accidental. For it is Outler's vision of evangelism that governs to a great degree what has happened in evangelism in much of United Methodism over the last forty years. We might say that Outler's ideas form a kind of background music that echo back and forth throughout United Methodism. Albert Outler was the crucial architect of United Methodism over the last forty to fifty years. This is best reflected in his role in the revisions on doctrine in the *Book of Discipline* in 1972. So he matters as the founding Father of our tradition in its most recent incarnation. Contemporary United Methodism stands to Albert Outler as the first generation of Methodism in England stood to John Wesley. His footprints are all over United Methodism, not least in our corporate thinking about evangelism. Hence it is surely vital that we look at his work on evangelism. In this regard we are extremely fortunate to have available not just his Denman Lectures[3] but also his volume of essays on evangelism.[4] Taken together, these provide a feast that are well worth sustained examination. Even then, we must proceed cautiously. We do not as yet have a critical biography of Outler's life and work.[5] More importantly, Outler is a very

[3] Happily still in print in Albert C. Outler, *Evangelism and Theology in the Wesleyan Spirit* (Nashville, Tenn: Discipleship Resources, 1996).

[4] Albert C. Outler and William J. Abraham, ed., *Evangelism: Essays by Albert Cook Outler* (Anderson, Ind: Bristol House, 1998). The whole corpus of his papers together with his books are a treasure trove of theological reflection.

[5] Bob W. Parrott, *Albert C. Outler: The Gifted Dilettante* (Anderson, Ind: Bristol House, 1999), is invaluable reading.

complex scholar; it is well-nigh impossible to do full justice to the subtlety of his proposals.

Outler was born on November 17, 1908 and died on September 1, 1989. Given that the Berlin Wall fell on November 9, 1989, we might say that his life spans the full course of the twentieth century understood as a unity. His wingspan intellectually was staggering; his interests were insatiable. There is a story out of Perkins that he once went fishing with Dean Joseph Quillian. When they got to a cement jetty, he was engrossed in working out the chemistry of the cement with one of the local fishermen. Quillian, it is said, vowed never to go fishing with him again.

His education at Wofford College, Emory, and Yale was deep and rigorous. There is no doubting his primary field of interest – he was a historian through and through – but beyond that he was a fox rather than a hedgehog, for he was ready to follow up any intellectual scent that was up for discussion. He always had a bibliography at the tip of his tongue in conversation. His intellectual interests went hand in hand with his commitment to the Church and to the Christian faith. I say Church with a capital C because, of course, his ecumenical endeavors were prodigious. Yet he never ceased to be a deeply committed Methodist both as a child and as an adult.[6] Thus his ecumenism was not a rootless or escapist ecumenism, it was an ecumenism grounded and expressed in his efforts to reshape Untied Methodism, to make it a denomination which was at once ecumenical and evangelical, both catholic and reformed. In and through all this he gave his life to the study of Wesley whom he clearly hoped to see enter the lists of great figures of Church history. Thus Wesley featured prominently in Outler's vision of evangelism in that Wesley was at the heart of his Denman Lectures.

Outler's interest in evangelism stretches back into the fifties, so we can look upon his take on Wesley as evangelist as the climax of his thinking on evangelism. This interest in evangelism was no mere footnote in his work as a whole. Indeed evangelism was inseparable from his vision of Christianity. He went so far as to insist, for example, that the theology of evangelism was simply the theology of Christianity. But we are moving

---

[6] Outler's Wikipedia entry describes him as "the first real United Methodist theologian," Wikipedia contributors, *Albert Outler*, (Wikipedia, The Free Encyclopedia)

http://en.wikipedia.org/w/index.php?title=Albert_Outler&oldid=459533948 (accessed February 18, 2012).

too fast, so let me set the table.

Outler's Vision of Evangelism

The core issue that shaped the heart of Outler's vision of evangelism was this: how do we articulate and share the Gospel in a world that has changed dramatically from the world we inherited? Nowhere is this stated more succinctly and dramatically than in his autobiographical comments in *The Christian Century* for February 3, 1960. He tells us there that he was born and reared in the eighteenth century, he passed through the nineteenth century in seminary, and that he converted to liberalism in the Great Depression. Going to Yale brought him into the twentieth century where he was clearly shaken to the foundations reading A. J. Ayer, Reinhold Niebuhr, and T. S. Eliot.[7] What really hit home was the problem of how to remain faithful to the continuous content of the Christian tradition down to the end of the

---

[7] Elsewhere (in a paper written while a graduate student at Yale) he tells us that he had been "...in turn a fundamentalist, then a radical, then a "social gospeler," an exponent of religion and nurture and education; and each of these has left its trace in the complex of his [my] beliefs." In Albert C. Outler and Leroy T. Howe, ed., *The Pastoral Psychology of Albert C. Outler* (Anderson, Ind: Bristol House, 1997), 27.

eighteenth century while at the same time taking seriously the Enlightenment of the modern period. It was in struggling with this tension that he found his vocation as a historian, namely, the challenge of how to trace the identity and continuity of historic Christianity across the ages. Thus his theological vocation meant "a double effort to comprehend the Christian tradition in its historic continuity and the modern world in its intellectual and spiritual ambiguities."[8] Theologically he expressed the issue in terms of anthropology and Christology. By the nineteenth century a master image of the human condition had captured the imagination: human agents on their own can redeem themselves. That master image of the nineteenth century was utterly destroyed by the First World War. The problem the new thinking about human agency initially raised still persisted for any church committed to evangelism. How do we develop "a modern doctrine of the Savior of modern sinners"? Or put differently: "…if a modern man is to witness to Jesus Christ as *his* Lord and Savior, what sort of language, derived from his noetic categories, can he rightly use to celebrate his new life with God in Christ?"[9]

---

[8] Parrott, *Albert C. Outler, The Gifted Dilettante*, 239.
[9] Ibid., 240.

We can detect here three elements that were vital to Outler's intellectual work as a theologian. First, there is a commitment to Jesus Christ as Lord. This was what remained as the core of the classical Christian tradition after the onslaught of criticism by its modern opponents and despisers running from the eighteenth to the twentieth century. Second, there is a privileging of contemporary neotic categories in any effort to bear witness to Christ as Lord. Here Outler displays his intense interest in the problems of apologetics, of theological method, of authority, and of the epistemology of theology. This came, of course, to its climax in the invention of the so-called Wesleyan Quadrilateral. Third, there is a sharp focus on new life as constitutive of the Christian life lived under the Lordship of Jesus Christ.[10] Interesting-

---

[10] We can hear these themes in another key in a passage describing an intellectual crisis that he underwent in college. After a sermon by a visiting theological professor during a religious emphasis week, he "… went out into the woods and faced out the problem as far as it would go. This was the conclusion: God must be real, even if I cannot apprehend him; Jesus Christ was all that I could conceive of love and goodness, and therefore all I could know and all I needed to know. In his way of living was all that I could ask of meaning, dignity, and heroism. All the alternatives were lesser ones, leading to a materialistic and vulgar code

ly, Outler picked up this theme of new life from the Buchmanites[11] rather than from Wesley,[12] but it may well explain the turn to Wesley as a critical source for Methodist theology and for evangelism in his later career.[13]

What was at issue, then, for Outler as a theologian was how to develop a vision of the Christian faith that would be a match for the situation in which he found himself in the twentieth century. This situation had long been a source of perplexity. By the 1960s, he saw doom and gloom all around him. The host of promises to fix the world without Christianity that had been trumpeted for over two centuries had fallen apart. Secular-

---

of values and conduct, however glossed with worldly prestige." Howe, *The Pastoral Psychology of Albert C. Outler*, 24-5.

[11] This group was also known as "the Oxford Group" and as "Moral Rearmament." It was founded and led by Dr. Frank Nathan Buchman (1871-1961), an American Lutheran minister. It was supported for a time by a network of British MPs. Its core belief was that God could change both individuals and the world.

[12] Howe, *The Pastoral Psychology of Albert C. Outler*, 28.

[13] Clearly there were political dimensions in the turn to Wesley, for Outler skillfully used his study of Wesley to rework Methodism in the direction that he felt was critical for its future health and survival.

ism, the idea that human agents could find happiness and flourish without God, had turned out to be a total crock. The intellectual alternatives to Christianity were no more persuasive than the core of Christian belief. The climax of secularist forms of faith, as represented by Harvey Cox and the Death of God theologians of the 1960s were a joke. Yet there was no turning the clock back. Many of the criticisms of orthodoxy and traditional Christianity were valid; the intellectual horizons of unbelief had to be honored. So the central task for theologians was to keep their nerve and hold on, then go back and recover as much of the great Christian tradition as was salvageable, and only then find a way to share that faith within the language and thought forms of the new and terrible day that had dawned.

Outler's Strategy for Evangelizing the Modern World

One extremely significant material result of this strategy comes out very forcefully in his single work of constructive theology, namely, his book on providence.[14] Outler clearly has his back

---

[14] Albert C. Outler, *Who Trusts in God; Musings on the Meaning of Providence* (New York: Oxford University Press, 1968).

against the wall in that volume. He is living in an intellectual world where the last vestiges of theism have been shredded. His reaction was forthright and many-sided. He has had enough of the criticisms of unbelief; he cannot believe for one moment that the secular alternatives will bring anything but disaster for the church and for society; he is fed up with theologians throwing in the towel; he is utterly determined to tackle the problem of God head-on; he even refuses to shirk the challenge of evil. Yet he works valiantly to try and meet the unbeliever in his or her demand for evidence on their own ground. It is not enough to parrot the faith of the past; we can no longer work with divine intervention and a god of the gaps; divine impassibility and immutability are out; the penal substitutionary theory of the atonement is a lost cause; original sin and total depravity no longer ring true; revivalism is finished; fundamentalism is fatally flawed.

Rather than simply parrot the faith of the past, we must now speak up for faith in the language of our contemporaries. He develops this option along the following lines. Our lives are surrounded by an irreducible mystery. That mystery is known in the life, death, and victory of Jesus Christ who is the paradigm representation of a

grace and power that operates at all levels of reality, that is, throughout nature and human history.
Human agents enjoy genuine freedom, a freedom
given continuously by God outside of our *chronos*
time but inside of *kairos* time. Unfortunately, we
have abused that freedom and now live in inescapable anxiety and inhumanity outside of grace.
We can only be turned the right way up by God.
In Jesus Christ we are called back to a faith and
trust that transforms us and the world. Through
faith we know the mystery that surrounds us as
the Triune God of Christianity. The only language
we have to express this mystery is apophatic and
parabolic, but we can look to the Holy Spirit to
aid us in making the faith alive in the language of
our contemporaries. The end result is a stout defense of the doctrine of providence. Within this
he readily deploys the insights of Process philosophy and of psychotherapy. He also uses every sinew of his intellectual and rhetorical ability
to make clear that he has sounded the depths of
modern culture.

What is fascinating about the content of Outler's book on providence is its theological thinness and its ambivalence. Outler has cut back the
faith fundamentally to a vision of providence.
"Providence is the sum of all the modes of God's

[his] self-disclosure in human history, of all the effects of his love in our hearts."[15] It is as if this is the last ditch that has to be defended after all else has been surrendered. This thinness, of course, is inevitable given his aggressive rejection of divine intervention in the world. This accounts in turn for the double ambivalence. On the one hand, Outler wants to hold on to a high Christology and to a robust vision of the Trinity. On the other hand, this takes us way beyond a vision of God that collapses all the forms of divine interaction with the world into one of provident presence. The commitment to Christology and the Trinity sits in contradiction to his vision of divine agency; incarnation and resurrection involve divine intervention, if anything does. Equally interesting, Outler loses his nerve when it comes to the problem of evil. On the one hand, he shifts back and forth between Irenaeus and Augustine, between John Hick and Austin Farrer. On the other hand he gives up in intellectual despair, before finally dropping the whole affair and diving headlong into a brilliant overview of the deep narrative of the whole sweep of scripture.[16] We

---

[15] Outler: *Who Trusts in God*, 79-80.

[16] He lamely announces at this point that "...a sort of homily must suffice – a sermon that begins with an

see here a mind caught in acute cognitive dissonance. On the one side, he has internalized the no-holds-barred attack on Christianity and has come to agree with much of it; on the other side, he is desperately trying to keep afloat and recover utterly core elements of the Christian tradition represented by scripture, Nicaea, and Chalcedon. When he runs into the sands on the problem of evil, he retreats to the exposition of scripture.

Outler's Proposals in Evangelism

All of this is vital for grasping the full force of Outler's vision of the theory and practice of evangelism. The same central methodological moves are in play. First, we must discern the essence of the Christian faith as it has survived across the cries of church history. Second, we must bear witness to that core in every aspect of the life of the church in the language and thought forms of our day and generation.

A close reading of Outler's work on evange-

amateur's reading of the problem in Scripture and that concludes with what I hope is an honest and relevant "application" of the biblical wisdom about "overcoming evil with good" as Christians have tested this in the course of life and in the face of death." Outler: *Who Trusts in God*, 91. This turns out, however, to be one of the very best sections of the whole book.

lism makes readily manifest the crucial outcome of this process. He returns again and again to such themes as divine presence and love, the Trinity and Incarnation, justification by faith, a human-divine relationship, being truly human, and gaining life's true meaning. These signal his proposals on the outcome of the faith. What I want to emphasize is less the outcome of the strategy than the strategy itself. Characteristically he casts his proposal in a rhetoric of a third alternative that avoids two extremes. Thus, to take one sample, he resolutely rejects archaism and modernism. In the case of archaism, folk insist that the Christian faith must be received, renewed, and traditioned in the form in which it was presented. This results in a rift between "the life of and world of faith and the life and world of historical existence, of science, technology, business, politics, and cultures. This way lies obscurantism or else its matching opposite, unbelief."[17] The other alternative is modernism, that is, the effort to update the Gospel in modern terms, at whatever the cost. This way leads to revisionism and secularism. Happily, for Outler, a third alternative is available

---

[17] Outler, *Evangelism: Essays by Albert Cook Outler*, 159

... in the notion of the actus tradendi, which involves the intellQuotationectual renewal of the Gospel, the conscious, careful, risky business of rethinking the Gospel in terms and categories relevant and meaningful to the thought forms of a "new age," but it is always working from the premise of the Gospel's identity, continuity and universality – Jesus Christ, the same yesterday, today and forever. The faith once for all traditioned to the saints...never was a form of words, never was a conceptual pattern, never was a system of doctrine (not even the doctrine of sola scriptura). It is instead, the relationship of responsive and responsible trust in God's grace and providence made possible and secure by God's grace and providence made possible and secure by God's redemptive and reconciling deed in Jesus Christ.[18]

In his Denman Lectures Outler makes exactly the same point in terms of the legacy of Wesley. Excoriating the mindset that wants to go back to the Bible or to the old-time religion, he calls for an engagement with modernity.

---

[18] Outler, *Evangelism: Essays by Albert Cook Outler*, 159. Notice how the language of scripture is explicitly subverted here. Outler has shifted from faith being delivered to the faith being traditioned.

...the modern world "is where it's at," right now and for the foreseeable future that we are responsible for. Our account of the perennial *euangelion* must be addressed to the[se] new dimensions of human self-consciousness – if modern men are to be evangelized. I say this in full awareness of my zealous advocacy of John Wesley as a prime, and still vital, resource for modern concerns in evangelism, for I am equally eager to make the point that it is Wesley himself who stands as the paradigm for me in the business of doing theology for the actual people who are out there to *hear* the Gospel – rather than as a sort of template of truth to be pressed down on the hearer's mind, regardless of his own perceptions. Pure doctrine as an end in itself was Wesley's way in the barren years; he learned better after Aldersgate and Bristol.[19]

---

[19] Albert C. Outler, *Evangelism and Theology in the Wesleyan Spirit* (Nashville, Tenn: Discipleship Resources), 63. This is exactly the strategy that governs Outler's approach to the study of Wesley's theology. "What I have been trying to suggest thus far is that Wesley was very much a man of his own time and yet also that his interest in the relevance of the perennial gospel in the constantly changing human situation is pertinent to our own efforts to update that same gospel and to relate it, as best we may, to the vast and

If I were asked to put a name to Outler's theological vision as a whole then I would describe it as a version of evangelical liberalism. It is a hodgepodge of vague Trinitarian doctrine coupled with a heavy stress on divine grace, human freedom, and justification by faith, all wrapped up in a soft version of existentialist humanism. The crucial point to observe is the theological method employed. This is where the Protestant liberalism is clearly evident.[20] You begin with some account of the enduring content of Christianity and then express that content in ways intelligible to the host culture you are seeking to evangelize. Not surprisingly, the criteria for assessment for the re-expressed content of the faith are constituted by the quadrilateral of scripture, tradition, reason, and experience. In this the continuity is captured by scripture and tradition, the updating by reason and experience. Outler's method and his epistemology of theology are Siamese twins; you cannot really have one without the other. Equally unsurprisingly Outler's vision dovetails with a vision of theological pluralism as consti-

---

radical crises of our times." Ibid., 83.

[20] It is easy to miss this because "liberalism" is a contested notion and because Outler constantly rails against various forms of "liberalism."

tutive for United Methodism, for both the core components of the faith and its revised updating are such that they cannot be nailed down in any substantial way.

Beyond all this Outler's proposals with respect to the concept of evangelism are schematic and underdeveloped. The defining activity of evangelism is that of communication. The Word of God communicated must be audible, visible, and winsome. The motivation for evangelism is gratitude. The frontline agents of evangelism are lay people rather than professional evangelists. The church of such lay evangelists must be a church of martyrs and servants. It will be a church catholic, evangelical, and reformed: catholic in its human outreach, evangelical in its spiritual up reach, reformed in its constant openness to change. The goal of evangelism is the same as the goal of all Christian ministries, namely, the arrival of God's kingdom as manifest in Christ, in the lives of individuals, in the life of the church, and in society at large. The social consequence of evangelism is an indirect social revolution, where believers transform the social order. The primary danger to avoid in evangelism is that of extremism as represented by fundamentalism and liberalism; such extremes can be avoided by the constant search for a centrist position on contested issues that would operate with conjunctives rather than disjunctives, with balanced polarities rather than monothematic slogans. The hope for a new day in evangelism is for there to be a new Pentecost, a Third Great Awakening, in which the current church will find a way to update the essence of the faith for the new world in which we find ourselves. "There will be no *Third* Great Awakening until we come to terms with the fact that the *Second* is over and done with."[21]

Three Cheers for Effort

We can all agree that Albert Outler was one of the foremost theologians of United Methodism over the last generation in terms of institutional and intellectual influence. The skills on display are self-evident: enormous reserves of historical learning, extraordinary rhetorical skill, boundless energy, a deep desire to face the truth, and an uncanny eye for humbug. We can also agree that the challenges he faced in the formation of United Methodism were utterly formidable, for he was confronted with a situation which can best be described as chaotic theologically and un-

[21] Outler, *Evangelism and Theology in the Wesleyan Spirit*, 43.

manageable institutionally. So we can well understand the restlessness and unease that were such marked features of the last two decades of his life. It is not sufficiently well known that he developed very significant second thoughts about his early aversion to orthodoxy, his take on the canonical doctrines of United Methodism, his presentation of the so-called Wesleyan Quadrilateral, and his understanding of ecumenism.

Equally we can appreciate Outler's contribution to the debate about evangelism. His Denman Lectures are surely landmark lectures in the series as a whole; his enthusiasm for evangelism was contagious; his efforts to grapple with the historical and normative aspects of the subject are at times intellectually riveting; and the critical disposition he brings to the discussion is indispensable. I want especially to draw attention to his success in securing the McCreless chair of evangelism at Perkins School of Theology. His defense of evangelism as a constitutive element in theological education was way ahead of its time and was developed in the teeth of concerted academic opposition.[22] I trust we are all sufficiently aware of our debts to Outler; so we can now face

---

[22] See the chapter "Evangelism at Perkins," in Outler, *Evangelism: Essays by Albert Cook Outler*, chap. 7.

the fresh challenge we meet in the church today. As I said earlier, Outler's footprints are all over United Methodism, not least in the ethos that governs our work in evangelism.

It is time, however, to get past the hagiography and the appropriate praise and start coming to terms with the stark realities that lie at the core of Outler's work. The really salutary fact to notice at the outset is this: it is that form of Methodism that was constructed under Outler's tutelage and watch which has suffered drastic decline over the last forty years. The correlation between the impact of Outler's proposals and decline is stark and unmistakable. Whether there is causation is another matter, of course, but it remains as more than a mere possibility, for Outler's central proposals continue to be the air we breathe. Any explanation of decline will have to be thoroughly complex. There is no one magic bullet that has caused decline. However, no account of the decline can ignore the impact of Outler's vision of evangelism over the last generation.

The Unresolved Problems

The problems in Outler's proposals are manifold; and they run very deep indeed. Despite his awareness of the assault on Christianity in the modern period, his proposals do not begin to take with radical seriousness the offense of the Gospel in all cultures. Despite all the grand talk about the necessity of prevenient grace, they do not begin to fathom the native hostility in the human heart due to sin. Despite his commitment to research and intellectual virtue, they are laced with polemical caricature, concealed dogmatism, and litanies of bogus alternatives. Despite his avowals of intellectual freedom, they represent one particular way of thinking about the Christian faith in the wake of modernity. Each of these concerns could be developed at length. In this lecture, however, I will limit myself to two salient criticisms.

First, Outler's proposals concerning the practice of evangelism are more rhetorical than they are substantial. While they do indeed provide a place for evangelism in the life of the church, they tend to collapse evangelism into whatever communicative practices enhance the faith as a whole rather than deal head on with the pivotal need to bring the Gospel to the world and then proceed to make disciples. Thus Outler limits evangelism to proclamation or witness and sets his face against the critical need for initiation into a robust version of Christianity. This is astonishing given his hearty sense of the long haul effects of two hundred years of relentless intellectual attack on Christianity in the West. If we are really in a radically changed situation where Christendom is over, where United Methodism has been sidelined culturally in the United States, where the secular alternatives have failed to deliver on their empty promises, then it is utterly imperative that we find the lost sheep, introduce them to the green pastures of the Gospel, and see to it that they are given the initial formation that will enable them to both survive in and make a real difference to the world. If Wesley felt it was imperative to do this in a world that was explicitly Christian and confessional, how much more so must we face this challenge in our world today? One recent survey of high school seniors reported that half of the students thought that Sodom was married to Gomorrah.[23] Outler was still living off the capital of the past, even though he knew the bank was running out of reserves. Thus the enormity of the challenge of evangelism escaped him. He did not see or take seriously the need for proper grounding in the faith for the first time as vital for any viable practice of evangelism in our

---

[23] See "Postcard: Winchester," *Time*, December 8, 2008, 10.

situation.

Second, his fundamental methodology is superficially attractive but ultimately disastrous for the theory and practice of evangelism. The strategy was simple: develop a vision of the core of Christianity and then express that within the conceptual and intellectual norms of the host culture. This is so much part of the air we breathe that folk take to it like a duck takes to water. After all, we want to be faithful to Christian identity, so let's make sure we have a core of faith to transmit. After all, we really do want to reach the world as it is, so we must step up and translate the faith into contemporary cultural idiom. Who could contest these obvious platitudes? However, these are not at all platitudes. They are thoroughly modern, contingent developments. And they are fatal to the practice of authentic and effective evangelism. Let me explain.

This strategy confuses the proper desire to understand and connect with contemporary culture with the radically different operation of translating the faith into the concepts and idiom of contemporary culture. Suppose for a moment that we have minimal agreement on what the core of the Gospel and the faith are. There are then two quite different sets of issues that we have to face in evangelism. First, there is the issue of how we justify the core truth claims of Christianity in the face of concerted incredulity, if not outright hostility. Second, there is the radically different issue of how we connect the claims we advance with the culture we currently inhabit. The latter challenge broadly is one of style: how do we meet people where they are in terms of time, space, music, code words, analogies, images, linguistic peculiarities, architecture, media, forms of communication, and the like? The former challenge broadly is one of philosophy: how do we deal with objections, provide warrant and justification, solve the problem of authority, give reasons for the hope within us, and the like. Outler gave up on the first enterprise; he simply did not have the resources to deal with the massive intellectual attack on Christianity launched by Hume, Kant, Nietzsche, Freud, Marx, Russell, Ayer, and Flew. So he collapsed these two enterprises and then opted for a solution of translation; the goal became that of making the core available in the idiom and conceptuality of contemporary culture. The aim was to translate the faith into the language of the university common room, the couch, and the country club. This was precisely why Outler turned to Process philosophy and psychotherapy. These represented the highbrow intellectual culture which Outler inhabited. If he had been trained in Germany he might have opted for Heidegger and existentialism, if in Britain for Wittgenstein and linguistic analysis, if in Latin America for Marx and socialism. This strategy, however, is a recipe for decline and death. It offers a woolly Christianization of contemporary highbrow cultural commitments in the name of faith. We can be sure that the contemporary norms of thought will swallow up the content of the faith.

This is already a problem when the culture is seen as parochial and monolithic, that is, Western and modern. In this instance the translation casts the faith into the categories of modern philosophy and psychotherapy. Once the culture becomes radically diverse and genuinely global, then the proposed translations simply become even more incommensurable and contradictory. Given that postmodern culture tends to abandon the quest for credibility as a nasty hallmark of modernity, the temptation to opt for a strategy of translation is even more acute. The whole idea of providing a justification for the truth claims of Christianity collapses as an exercise in intellectual tyranny. So all that remains is the problem of how to connect with the contemporary culture; the move to translation is almost inevitable given the options available. The outcome, however, is exactly the same. The Christian Gospel and faith become hostage to the host culture. Communication of the Gospel ends up being the echo of our own interests, social location, political commitments, and cultural ideologies. In these circumstances the Gospel itself gets reworked as a representation of the ideology of diversity and inclusivism. The task of the theologian is to provide an apologetic for this reconstruction of the Christian faith.

For Outler then, what the Gospel cannot be is the radical Good News of the arrival of the Kingdom of God to the Jew first and then to the Gentile, for every attempt to state the Gospel is essentially the product of our cultural location. Spiritual formation cannot involve substantial initiation into the canonical faith of the Church, for even to identify the faith of the Church will be seen as the arbitrary and hegemonic option of one party trying to drown out other voices. Evangelism cannot be rooted and grounded in special revelation as enshrined in the faith of the Church, for the purpose of revelation is not the gracious disclosure of truth but an invitation to a pious silence and a noisy humility.

The Tragic Outcome

The overall outcome of Outler's strategy across forty years can now be stated simply. The Church becomes an endless seminar in search of elusive and ultimately unattainable truth, rather than the carrier of the rich and salutary faith once delivered to the saints. United Methodist scholars and leaders have given up on any serious intellectual defense of the faith, opting instead for the quest for the culturally relative translation that will somehow take us through to the next generation. Any effort to have a concerted, church-wide, united practice of evangelism is doomed to failure because there is no common faith. Any proposal to this end will be evaluated not in terms of the Gospel of Jesus Christ but in terms of a new Gospel of diversity and inclusivism. The practice of evangelism, understood as a specific and vital ministry of the church, is folded into the more generic field of discipleship; the term evangelism is then used in a Pickwickian manner to cover anything remotely related to that elusive concept. The Gospel itself becomes a game of smoke and mirrors. We might say that the Word of God becomes the hearsay of the internet; the Wisdom of God becomes the foolishness of the intellectual elite or of populist pundits; the Kingdom of God is reduced to a television slogan of Open hearts, Open minds, Open doors; the wine of faith is turned into insipid, bottled water; the body and blood of Christ are turned into stale memories and images, the mere corpse of some recently invented Jesus of history. No church can survive more than two to three generations as an effective agent of evangelism once this happens; it is a case of death by our own hands delivered in the name of evangelism.

I mentioned, however, that Outler himself towards the end of his life had very serious reservations about some of the crucial proposals he developed in the 1960s and 70s. Thus he had second thoughts about orthodoxy, about the content of the canonical doctrines of United Methodism, about the quadrilateral, and about ecumenism. Unfortunately, little if anything is known about these second thoughts outside a very small academic network. All of these are relevant to my concerns here, but I want to pick up on only one of them, namely, the shift in ecumenism. In this instance he turned to the topic of pneumatology as vital to any future prospects for the unity of the Church. How might this help in evangelism? The work of the Spirit shows up, of course, in his reflections on evangelism. He insisted that the work of the Holy Spirit was vital in the genesis of faith. He cast a curious eye over the arrival of the Charismatic movement as seen within the Roman Catholic tradition.[24] In fact he looked for a new Pentecost, a Third Great Awakening. But what might happen if we picked up on Pentecost and pneumatology as pivotal in evangelism. Would this help us in thinking through how we might move into a whole new era where our approach to evangelism could be reconstructed so as to bypass the problems that show up in Outler's work and in the last generation? It is this question that I shall take up in my next lecture.

---

[24] It did not appear that he had any interest in the arrival of the Charismatic movement within United Methodism. Perhaps it was too close to home and maybe in his eyes too close to the evangelical wing of the church at a time when he was very unsure of its value.

2. Chinese Fireworks

Introducing John Sung

In my last lecture I looked at the significance of Albert Outler's vision of evangelism and the impact that vision has had on United Methodism over the last generation. In this lecture I want to explore and examine a very different approach to the theory and practice of evangelism. I dare to believe that if Outler were here, he would be sympathetic to what I shall present, for it is clear that he had serious misgivings about several of the proposals that were dear to his heart when he was at the height of his powers. Like Augustine, one of his heroes, he was not afraid to write retractions, even though many of his disciples are so enamored with his earlier work that they have missed this completely. I have been especially intrigued by Outler's turn to the life and work of the Holy Spirit as vital to any future vision of church unity. This dovetails very nicely with his musings about a new Pentecost in the life of the church which shows up in his reflections on evangelism. Thus he raises the question of a Third Great Awakening in his third Denman Lecture.

So in this second lecture I want to explore the life and work of an extraordinary evangelist called John Sung. I shall begin by developing a rich overview of his life, then summarize his vision of evangelism (with suitable explanatory commentary), and finish by highlighting the issues his life and vision raise for us today.

John Sung was born in China in 1901 and died in China in 1944. In all he lived for forty three years, yet he is often identified as the greatest Chinese evangelist of the twentieth century.[25] Several considerations make him a figure of great interest for these lectures: he was born and died a Methodist; he spent seven years in America where he earned a doctorate in chemistry from Ohio State University; he was exposed to the same kind of

---

[25] See Michael D. Suman, *The Church in China, One Lord Two Systems* (Kothanur, Bangalore: SAIACS Press), 156.

intellectual challenges that Outler catalogues in his journey; and his work in evangelism clearly bears the watermark of his formation in the Methodist tradition. What sets him apart are the depth of his faith, the ferocity of his passion for evangelism, and – most importantly – the exploration of avenues of the work of the Spirit that are mostly a deep embarrassment to modern, mainline Christianity. It is no surprise that his life and work were initially forgotten but, when rediscovered, manifest insights and developments that are now commonplace in Third World Christianity.

John Sung was born Sung Shang Chieh in Hong Chek Village, Putian, in the Province of Fujian.[26] He was also known by the name of Tian

---

[26] The main source for what follows is Shangjie Song and Levi Sung, *The Journal Once Lost: Extracts from the Diary of John Sung* (Singapore: Genesis Books, 2008). A later revised edition is now also available, Shangjie Song, Levi Sung, and Pheng Soon Thng, *The Diary of John Sung: Extracts from His Journals and Notes* (Singapore: Genesis Books, 2012). I have also benefited from Leslie T. Lyall, *A Biography of John Sung*, and William E. Schubert, *I Remember John Sung*, both published as one volume under the title of *John Sung: A Biography of John Sung* (Singapore: Armour Pub, 2005). For a fine overview of his life see Ka-Tong Lim, *The Life and Ministry of John Sung* (Singapore: Genesis Books, 2012).

En. His father, Sung Lian Xue, was a Methodist pastor, a man with an oddball temperament that he passed on to his son. He was reared in poverty. The church too was poor, but not poor in spirit, for they were visited with seasons of revival that had a deep impact on the young John Sung growing up. So much so that as a boy and teenager he earned the title of "The Little Pastor." By a stroke of good fortune he was offered a scholarship to attend Ohio Wesleyan University in 1920, graduating on June 13, 1923, with a degree in chemistry. From there he moved to Ohio State University where he earned in succession his M.Sc. in 1924 and his Ph.D. in 1926. During that time he worked double shifts to pay his way through school, developed hemorrhoids for which he never got effective treatment,[27] became a natural student-body leader, and spoke from time to time in local Methodist churches. He even formed an evangelistic band to preach to country churches in the area. In 1925 he was given a "Preacher's License" in Indiana.

Sung initially came to Ohio to study theology, but switched to science possibly because of misgivings about the faith he had already picked

---

[27] He had to deal with extensive bleeding and bouts of searing pain for most of his ministry.

up in China. China had seen an influx of secular thinking represented by John Dewey and Bertrand Russell, a development that no doubt paved the way for the radical secularism of the communist regime that arrived under Mao much later. Whatever may have been the case, Sung remained a Christian through his studies. Towards the end he was told by the Rev. Wilbur Fowler of the local Wesley Foundation that he looked far more like a preacher than a scientist. This must have stirred an earlier sense of calling, for he enrolled in Union Theological Seminary, New York, in the Fall of 1926 and remained there till February 1927. At the time Union was one of the leading seminaries of North America; it was in full bloom as a bastion of progressive, liberal Christianity as represented by the great orator and preacher, Harry Emerson Fosdick. It is hard not to believe that John Sung entered Union with high hopes and expectations. His prayer en route was: "Lord, may the rivers of living water cascade from within my heart into a never-ending stream."[28] Yet this betokened no narrow sensibility: he had in fact chosen Union because of its proximity to Columbia University, a place which would allow him to broaden his knowledge of other fields.

---

[28] Levi, *The Journal Once Lost*, 39.

The Experience at Union Seminary, New York

The events that unfolded at this point are fascinating. Union turned out to be a bitter disappointment. Spiritual life was at low ebb. In the study of scripture and evangelism, whatever science had failed to prove was dismissed as incredible and unreasonable. For a time Sung took shelter in a version of the social Gospel, branding the more conservative believers as emotional, superstitious, and muddle-headed. He starting skipping lectures, began exploring his native Chinese religions, and ended up at times chanting Buddhist scriptures.[29] Over time he gave up any residual faith he had in the Bible and toyed with the idea of starting his own religion. In the end he entered a state of confusion and total darkness. His life, his faith and his mental state were clearly shattered.

Then, just before Christmas 1926, Sung attended an evangelistic meeting with several friends. The preacher was a 15-year-old girl dressed in white from head to toe. His friends later were bristling with criticism and charged that she offered nothing but emotive superstition. Sung was

---

[29] He even translated the *Daode Jing* by Laozi into English.

taken aback both by the power and crispness of her message and by the spiritual atmosphere of the meeting, so much so that he went back four times. Sung did not respond immediately to the messages he heard; he pondered them deeply as he read various Christian biographies during the winter vacation. He had been smitten by a vision of New Life and power that attracted him. Over time he came through to a whole new faith.

His diary at this point needs to be quoted in full.

> The New Year's Eve of 1926 saw me kneeling down in fervent prayer when God spoke to me in the Spirit: "I will destroy the wisdom of the wise; the intelligence of the intelligent I will frustrate." (1 Corinthians 1:19) These words were spoken gently, in a still small voice. What is so great about man's knowledge and capabilities? I could not sleep and felt anxious that night until the dawn of 1 January 1927.
>
> As the days passed, my spirit was so weighed down by sin that I felt no peace. On the night of 10 February 1927, I wept and prayed in desperation. From about ten o'clock that night, the scenes of my own sinful life played out before my very eyes, even those hidden ones, and the protagonist was

none other than myself! I recalled that there was a copy of the New Testament Bible right at the bottom of a chest. I dug it out and flipped open Luke 23. I felt as though my spirit had floated out of my body and was following Jesus, with the cross on His back, as He walked to Golgotha. I could also feel the weight of my manifold sins almost crushing me to death.

There was the Lord, hanging up high on the Cross and blood was oozing out from His hands. What a tragic sight to behold! I dropped on my knees in humility, and pleaded with the Lord to cleanse me with His precious Blood from all unrighteousness. Then the Lord said, "Son, your sins are forgiven!" I looked up at His face that was glowing with light and the marks on His hands, and He added, "You must change your name to John." The Lord explained that it was John the Baptist who had prepared the way for the Lord and made straight the paths for Him. When the Lord comes again, He will choose me as one of His heralds. I am to proclaim the message, "The Kingdom of God is at hand, and the Lord is coming."

It was one o'clock in the morning and my body was aching all over, yea, every inch of it: my bones, sinews, innards and all. I felt as though I was suffering from a major injury. The Lord was reminding me and helping me understand what it was like to be crucified with Him.

The series of visions that I witnessed that night reeled into seven volumes. It started with knowing the truth about my own sins and ended with my call from the Lord. Then, it was daybreak.

Soon, I was boldly testifying to everyone I met about what God had done for me the night before, knowing full well that I would be mocked at for this. But that was the least of my concerns.[30]

Consequent to this experience John Sung began to witness in a whole new way to the faith. At times he would burst into singing in joy or humming in sorrow. Many people at Union seminary thought he was out of his mind. One week later on 17 February, 1927, he came back to the seminary only to find the gate closed in his face. The principal told him to follow a man, who then took him to a well-known psychiatric hospital, Bloomingdale Hospital, where he was admitted to Ward X, Block 4. Earlier in the evening he had seen two boys scrawl the word "rest"

---

[30] Levi, *The Journal Once Lost*, 42-3.

on the road, which was exactly what the doctor proposed that he should do. He remained at Bloomingdale for 193 days, during which time he read through the Bible forty times, each time using a different scheme of study. He tried escaping, but was caught by police dogs and brought back to a more secure ward. He fell into despair, but regained his nerve when God reassured him that all things do really work together for good. In the end after medical friends, Dr. Wu and his wife, agreed to be his guardian, and after the Chinese government made inquiries about what was happening, he was released from Union on condition that he would leave the country.[31] He stopped off with the Wu family in Cincinnati and eventually sailed from Seattle on 11 October, 1927. On the way home he disposed of all his Western medals and degrees except for his Ph.D. diploma that he kept for the sake of his father.

Ministry in China

John Sung spent the rest of his life in China and

---

[31] The Chinese consul later told William E. Schubert when the latter asked him if Sung was a little bit "off": "No, Mr. Schubert, he was no more crazy than you or I, but he had such a good case of real, old-fashioned religion, and it was so unusual there, they thought he was crazy." See Lyall and Schubert, *John Sung*, 250-1.

neighboring countries. He married, spent six months in teaching, and then embarked on an itinerant ministry that lasted until his death in 1944. During the Christophany at Union in which he received his call, he was also given a vision in which his life was divided into five three-year periods.[32] Each period was marked by a symbol. For the first period the symbol was water representing his return to China. The second symbol was a door, signaling the opening of his ministry beyond his own province, Fujian. The third symbol was a dove, signaling with a time of an unusual outpouring of the Spirit when there were in the region of 100,000 converts. The symbol for the fourth was blood, representing both the blood of warfare and the blood issuing from Sung's fistula and hemorrhoids. This led into the fifth and final period, signaled by a tomb. In this time he was confined to his home in Peking where he sometimes held three meetings a day, lying in bed. Before he died, he prophesied to a close associate that the Chinese church would go through a period of trial by fire, that the missionaries would be forced to leave, but that beyond that there would a great revival in China. He died on 18 August, 1944, after contracting tuberculosis and is buried

---

[32] Lyall and Schubert, *John Sung*, 258-9.

in Fragrant Hills, Peiping (Beijing).

Sung's ministry spanned a fifteen year period. His impact is such that he is still fondly remembered by believers in Singapore and Malaysia who were the beneficiaries of his ministry. Those that I have met in person speak of him in awe. Yet he was a rough character, ferocious in his passion for souls to the point where he neglected his family and really became a workaholic. He was outspoken in his criticisms of missionaries, aroused opposition from the authorities, and had a one track mind so that he did not always suffer fools gladly. He once lost his temper in the pulpit at a Quaker service because there were so many extraneous elements in the liturgy. He worked inside and outside of the Methodist system. He was not interested in the daily newspaper and refused to read the Conference course books because they had "no taste."[33] He got rebaptized as an adult. At times he ran into opposition from local Methodist ministers and bishops; most of the time the relationship was thoroughly positive. He was committed to the ministry of women, recruiting them as evangelists. He steered clear of local and

---

[33] Schubert tells us he was admitted to the Hingwa Conference anyway. Lyall and Schubert, *John Sung*, 281.

national politics, but he had a finely honed sense
of justice and equality. He was committed to the
theological education, though he worried about
the danger of superficiality and spiritual barren-
ness that might result from bad theological education.

Sung's Vision and Practice of Evangelism

Sung did not develop any explicit theory of evangelism. Yet we can readily discern the contours
of his vision of evangelism from his practices
and from the reports that are available. As a way
into a summary of his theory and a commentary
upon it, it is important to note that Sung clearly
believed that the office of evangelist was the foundation of the ministry of evangelism in the life of
the church. Here he differs radically from Outler
who excoriated evangelists with such vehemence
that it reached the level of contempt.[34] Clearly the

---

[34] Outler saw a long list of distinguished evangelists
from Paul to Billly Graham, which he studied for a
course at Perkins, as psychologically dysfunctional.
"The whole group of men we studied, my wild-fire
brethren of the tabernacles, present the evidence that,
by nature, they were aggressive, opinionated, ma-
nipulaters, puppeteers, the hero in their own illustra-
tions, obsessive-compulsive men, strongly erotic and
cocky – but, as often as not, cocky by being boastfully

source of Sung's position stems from his own call to the office. Here the great hero was John Wesley. He once stated that China needed five John Wesleys.[35] His other heroes were Charles Finney, D. L. Moody, and Evan Roberts. Sung's vision of evangelism was deeply shaped by his interpretation of these figures.

The primary practice of evangelism was that of proclamation aimed at a clear verdict for or against the Gospel. Thus Sung picked up on the standard practice of altar calls and the lifting of hands as a way of indicating a response to the call to repentance and faith. He also kept a close eye on the numbers of converts. He was not above gimmicks.[36] Yet evangelism did not end with the

---

humble. In short, these men, by *nature* belonged to what psychologists have defined as "the authoritarian personality" and been commonly reckoned as unhealthy characters to whose influence they trace a good deal of the religious psychopathology they see in their work in psychotherapy." See Outler and Abraham, ed., *Evangelism: Essays by Albert Cook Outler*, (Anderson, Ind: Bristol House, 1998), 61. Emphasis as in the original.

[35] Levi, *The Journal Once Lost*, 286.

[36] He printed imitation checks registered with the Bank of Heaven using Philippians 4:19 and writing in 100,000 souls as the amount to be paid by the bank on 22 March, 1932. See Levi, *The Journal Once Lost*, 185,

numbers of decisions made, for Sung sought to provide for adequate follow-up in terms of instruction and spiritual support. Thus he formed evangelistic bands that engaged in both proclamation and the provision of fellowship for new believers or for reinvigorated nominal Christians. In 1930 he established 1,000 house churches. Sung also attended to the needs of his converts in a more personal manner. He asked those who came to him for spiritual help to write out their requests and include with that request a photograph. These letters became the basis of his prayers for them when he would rise early in the morning to intercede.

We can see in all of this the reappropriation of the practices of Wesley, readjusted in the wake of the revivalist tradition, and cast in a way that would fit into the situation in China. We might think of his practice of evangelism as a combination of proclamation, altar call, and organized follow-up. This captures the heart of the matter. We need, however, extensive commentary to get the full force of this conventional vision of evangelism. The great danger on our part in hearing this is familiarity and superficiality.

---

for a photocopy.

Sung was flexible and innovative in this cluster of practices. The content of his preaching focused on lively exposition of Scripture. This began with his immersion in scripture when he was in Bloomingdale Hospital. Thereafter he could be found reading eleven chapters of scripture on a daily basis. Yet his delivery was tailored to his hearers. Thus he used visual aids, reproduced the message in popular songs, and invented relevant skits. He broke up his sermons by the use of choruses that captured the main point of the scriptures he was expounding. On some occasions he would ask those in the service to call out their favorite scripture chapters, write the results up on a blackboard, ask them to vote, and then preach on the chapter that got the most votes. He also used the Socratic method of question and answer, inviting participation in the reading and internalizing of scripture. It was common for him to preach three times a day. The sermons lasted up to two hours; at the end of the day Sung was exhausted, with his clothes soaked in sweat.

As to the message he preached, it is clear that he rambled all over scripture. In one short term Bible course he covered fourteen books in nineteen days. But he appears to have circled around themes that dealt with issues related to Christian initiation and the Christian life. One sermon, for example, centered on the following network of themes: repentance and new birth, dedication and holiness, obedience and the infilling of the Holy Spirit, working with joy for the Lord, experiencing living waters flowing eternally, bearing the Cross for the Lord and redeeming the debt of the Gospel, and enduring trials that foster faith.[37] We can be sure that these themes were set in the wider horizon of the salvation secured for all in the cross and resurrection of Christ.

As to the issue of the practice of altar calls, these were taken very seriously. On some occasions, Sung would gather the inquirers together after the rest had left, lock the doors, and then begin a period of intense interrogation and confession. He would call out a list of sins and invite those who had committed them to stand publicly. Some of the lists were drawn from the Free Church Common Liturgy of Confession. He would then call for repentance and for restitution where appropriate. After that he would lead in a prayer of forgiveness and sing a closing hymn. The results of this practice were solid conversions, many recommitments, and lasting faithfulness.

---

[37] Levi, *The Journal Once Lost*, 408.

Sung was acutely aware of the temptations that went with the work of an itinerant evangelist. He identified the besetting vices as fame, money, and lust. He also thought that the triad of fear, doubt, and worry were serious impediments in the work of evangelism. He worried at times about his impatience and his critical attacks on other pastors. Noting that the criticism of pastors had caused hearers to stumble rather than lead them to repentance, he recorded in his diary:

> I felt deep within me that I had merely criticized or analyzed the issues at stake even though I had given up everything, had fire in my belly and brought many people to the Lord. I lack the patience that had transformed Saul into Paul. While burning with love for the human soul, I had failed to be more understanding of the weaknesses of these people. I did not know how to use gentle acts of love to heal and bandage their gaping wounds, transforming them in the process.[38]

This sentiment dovetails with an outline of a sermon based on John 21, where he unpacks the dialogue between Peter and the Risen Lord on the importance of love in ministry. For Sung, love

---

[38] Levi, *The Journal Once Lost*, 273-4.

is essential to the feeding of Christ's lambs; the greater the love, the greater will be the work.[39]

Sung ends that same sermon with a plea for love and unity.

> You are a pastor and these followers are your brothers and sisters. It is only when you show love that you can feed the church. Moses led 600,000 people out of Egypt and yet they cursed him. The church is not working as one because there is no love. Paul went through great hardship to save his brothers and sisters because he loved them. The Lord shed His Blood and died on the Cross for our sake. Are we [you] willing to carrying (sic) the Cross for the Lord and take care of the church.[40]

This concern for unity in the church shows up on a host of occasions as essential to effective evangelism. Thus a plea for unity was once coupled with a hearty plea for repentance and radical self-emptying so that the power of God might be present in the church.[41]

---

[39] Ibid., 429-32.

[40] Levi, *The Journal Once Lost*, 432.

[41] Speaking of the church in which he was preaching but where there was corruption in the management of the finances by the pastor, he wrote: "I feel like the church is like the filament in a light bulb. There must

The Importance of Pentecost

It is very clear that Sung was intoxicated with the place of the Holy Spirit in his own life and ministry. Writing of the qualifications for preaching he notes that

> …knowledge and capability are not of prime importance in ministry work. What is crucial, rather, is to experience new life and be empowered by the Holy Spirit. The preacher with these two qualities versus one without produces results that are as different as precious stones are from withered grass.[42]

For Sung, the power of the Holy Spirit did not show up in a vacuum; the operation of the fullness of the Holy Spirit required radical repentance on the part of the preacher, a casting aside of self, and a personal openness to the Spirit. Once the Holy Spirit was present in power, then other gifts began to flow. A repeat of Pentecost and a whole

---

be a vacuum within so that the filament can light up when a current is passed through. It will not light up if there is air within. Abraham was a lamp; the Lord had spent decades to "siphon off the air within the bulb" so that he could shine. The church must first empty itself of sin before it can shine for the Lord." Levi, *The Journal Once Lost*, 71.

[42] Levi, *The Journal Once Lost*, 66.

new vision of ecclesiology then became possible.

This hope in a fresh Pentecost was no mere speculation. One of Sung's converts was a woman named Han Ai Guang. She was the widow of a military officer of great wealth and influence. Her husband kept two concubines. She lived the life of the vain and the rich, but when her son died she became mentally deranged. When her husband died, her life disintegrated, and she developed a serious bone disease. During this time she was converted through John Sung, took up theological studies at The Shanghai Far East Theological Seminary, and then, on the night of 30 December, 1934, she had a call to spread the Gospel in Yunnan. The record of a meeting in Sha Qiao led by Han Ai Guang then continues:

> The Holy Spirit came down on the third day, and some people saw tongues of fire descending from Heaven onto their church building. The entire congregation wept in repentance and the Lord performed many great miracles through her. She spent 10 years in Sha Qiao, where she led 3,600 people to the Lord.[43]

Sung's advice to Han Ai Guang in Sha Qiao is fas-

---

[43] Levi, *The Journal Once Lost*, 420.

cinating: "You must trust the Lord and establish His church on the same foundation as the times of the Apostles, because churches like these are rare nowadays."[44]

Given Sung's interest in Pentecost it is no surprise that Sung experienced the gifts of tongues and healing in his own ministry, or that these gifts showed up in his meetings. There are many reports of miraculous healing, so much so that these became something of a theological and practical problem. For one thing, he himself continued to suffer from constant bleeding; yet he was never healed. He resolved the dilemma by interpreting this as God's way of keeping him humble and dependent. It also showed that the power to heal belonged to God rather than to John Sung. The other problem was directly related to evangelism. People would exaggerate the significance of miracles, or they would turn to God because of miracles and then reject him when beset by trouble. Many of the letters he received showed much more concern for physical healing than for spiritual cleansing. There was little he could do about this other than seek to persuade them that miracles were utterly secondary to the cen-

---

[44] Ibid.

tral benefits provided in the Gospel and the work of the Holy Spirit. What was at issue for Sung at this point was the primary emphasis on deliverance from sin. This showed up in the capacity of the Holy Spirit to turn around people who were involved in such activities as idol-worship, gambling, opium addiction, womanizing, stealing, arson, killings, and the service of evil spirits. Here Sung expected full deliverance, with the limiting case calling for exorcism.

The Challenge Posed by Sung

While we began our analysis with the simple proposition that for Sung evangelism was constituted by proclamation, altar call, and follow-up, we can see that this is no mere rerun of a conventional vision of evangelism with which we are so familiar and against which mainline churches have generally recoiled. It is a radical and intense updating of that legacy to fit the Chinese situation. Evangelism, as seen in Sung's life and work, is concerned with communicating the Gospel accurately and effectively plus the invitation to faith and the development of the first phase of Christian discipleship. We might say that evangelism is proclamation plus catechesis. But Sung found a way to contextualize this vision of evangelism that was apt and truly functional.

Evangelism, on this analysis, is a specific ministry of the church that focuses on Christian initiation. It should not therefore be confused with the ongoing task of Christian nurture or the full-scale development of Christian discipleship. Nor should it be confused with the generic idea of witness, for everything we do is witness, whether good, bad, or indifferent. Nor should it be confused with church growth, for church growth does not in and of itself indicate that we have appropriate spiritual commitment. Moreover, evangelism understood in this way is no casual ministry. Evangelism is not a ministry that should be left to the crazies, the fainthearted, the ignorant, the emotionally unstable, or the spiritually immature. It requires costly sacrifice, deep compassion for the lost, intense intercession, flexible methods, the capacity to withstand hostile opposition, and serious personal engagement. Failure on any of these fronts will have serious consequences.

It is also clear that evangelism on this analysis is intimately related to a firm grasp of the Gospel, a robust vision of Christian initiation, and radical openness to the Holy Spirit. In other words, evangelism requires the very best theological judgment we can muster. It cannot be carried out for very long without substantial doctrinal commitments which are either hammered out in practice or handed down through a healthy doctrinal tradition. As to the Gospel, Sung was especially fortunate in that he was exposed to the Gospel as a child, had faced the rigors of a scientific training in chemistry, and finally came through to a deep understanding of repentance, the cross, and the power of the Holy Spirit in his experience at Union Seminary. He had also come to a deep appreciation of the power of prayer and of providence long before he came to Ohio. The same might be said of the formation of John Wesley, Sung's great hero. As to his theology, Sung pretty much made up his theology in guest houses, just as Wesley made up his theology on horseback. Yet Sung benefited enormously from the heritage he had inherited within Methodism, just as Wesley benefited from the heritage he received within Anglicanism. However, the acute problem Sung faced was that by the time he received it the Methodist heritage was already disintegrating. Thus Sung had no access, for example, to Wesley's critically important canonical sermons, precisely the material which would have served him so well in arriving at a model account of Christian initiation.[45]

This is where his story intersects with our own close to a century later, for despite thirty years of work on John Wesley, we too do not have access to Wesley's canonical sermons. What we have is an edition of the sermons by historians for historians, where what Wesley actually historically gave us was a carefully chosen set of sermons by an evangelist for evangelists. Worse still, United Methodism is *de facto* a fragmented collection of theologies developed from a weak epistemology that readily sanctions virtually any and every version of the Christian faith. We have turned the church from an Upper Room into an eternal seminar room. Hence we are incapable of reaching agreement on either the Gospel or a theology that would undergird the Gospel. In these circumstances we are right back with Sung and Wesley. Each of us has to make it all up as we go along. We have at best only sporadic, serendipitous ecclesial support. Consequently, we gravitate to this or that group or caucus inside the church for comfort and stimulus. This means that drop-

---

[45] I have in mind here the forty four sermons that were canonized in British Methodism. For the importance of these see my *Wesley for Armchair Theologians* (Louisville, Ky: Westminster John Knox Press, 2005).

ping Sung into the conversation is like lighting up a dazzling and dangerous Chinese firecracker. At best we are thrilled with the fireworks; at worst we are terrified that our church might catch fire and burn down.

For those who are worried that the church might catch fire, the vindication of Sung's vision of evangelism would be a real challenge. *Prima facie* Sung has been vindicated; or, better expressed, crucial features of his experiment in evangelism have been vindicated. Sung's vision of evangelism is initially vindicated by his dramatic call to engage in this kind of work. How can we turn our backs on what God is patently doing in our midst? This dovetails with the clear account of the place of evangelists as a specific ministry in the New Testament period, in the history of the early church, and in the lives of countless evangelists down through the history of the church. It is also vindicated by the needs of seekers; they are looking for help on what the faith really is and how to become a Christian. Sung is also vindicated by his success as one of the great evangelists of China in the twentieth century. This in turn correlates with the resounding success of the church in China and in the Third World. In this regard Sung and other unsung heroes have left a legacy that is absolutely astonishing, given the challenges they faced.[46] Closer to home, it is this kind of Christianity that is the source of the renewal of Methodism in Korea, Costa Rica, Cuba, Singapore, and Malaysia, to name but five Methodist churches which have been radically turned around in the last generation.

Making Sense of Sung's Proposals

By this stage those who like the Chinese firecracker are aglow with enthusiasm; those who are terrified have already called the fire brigade to put out the fire. It is time to calm down, to turn down the heat, and to keep our wits about us. We need to deal with the worries of those who have called the fire brigade. We can express our main worry in one of two ways. First, Sung sounds like a recipe for theological and ecclesiastical disaster. We are now loaded down with visions, speaking in tongues, exorcisms, and healings. We seem to enter a Protestant underworld of high octane supernaturalism, independent itinerant preachers, ad hoc theological experiments, sexual scandals,

---

[46] See Robert Aikman, *Jesus in Beijing: How Christianity Is Transforming China and Changing the Global Balance of Power* (Washington, DC: Regnery Pub, 2003), for a helpful overview.

financial mismanagement, and culturally illiterate leaders. Those who want that, it will be said, should leave and join the Pentecostals. Secondly, and more charitably, we are worried that Sung, despite his scientific credentials and his undoubted success, will undermine crucial elements in our Methodist heritage, not least our commitment to reason and experience. How should we respond to this concern? How should we assess Sung's life and work from this angle?

En route to answering these questions, we have to deal with Sung's interpretation of his experience at Union Seminary. Sung found initially that the teaching at Union stripped him of the faith of his youth and student days. This in turn led to the brink of spiritual disaster, leaving him in a state of confusion and total darkness. He then encountered the fifteen-year-old female preacher who rekindled his faith which led in time to his Christophany, his call, his visions of the future, his repentance, and the rebirth of his faith. Sung was dealing with a vision of the Christian faith that had eliminated anything that could not be shown by the methods of science. The seminary had bet the store on science, philosophy, and psychology as partners in reworking the faith and ministry of the church to fit a new era of world history. As

Sung nicely put it as applied to scripture, the rule for interpretation was simple: interpret scripture with science rather than the power of God.[47] In practice this naturally led to the ridiculing of the young female preacher as preaching emotive superstition. More dramatically, it meant that Sung's experience of God would be interpreted as a nervous breakdown, requiring that he be locked up and kept there until a way could be found to pack him back to China.

Sung reacted vehemently to the Liberal version of Protestantism he encountered at Union. His aversion to Union Liberalism shows up again and again in his diaries. He rails against its presence among western missionaries in China, so much so that he prays that God will take them home. He shows contempt for its superficiality in dealing with the depths of evil as expressed in its social Gospel. He laments over its capacity to destroy faith for it had no understanding of new birth or holiness. "Only the Liberals can destroy our faith where science and social service [had] failed to do so."[48] He is convinced that the church-

---

[47] This is taken from a list of eight theses that Sung associated with Liberalism. See Levi, *The Journal Once Lost*, 40.
[48] Ibid., 117.

es and organizations set up by Liberals could not withstand persecution; they were unreliable. "Only the churches set up by the Chinese and moved by the Holy Spirit would receive blessings from God."[49] At one point he goes so far as to tell a group of preachers "to make a commitment not to accept or spread the poison of Liberal beliefs."[50]

Vehement reactions are a dangerous development; very often we become the mirror images of those we oppose. So Sung was flirting with disaster in coming to terms with his experience at Union. He could easily have become a fighting fundamentalist who spent the rest of his days nurturing his gloomy conservative instincts, railing against the establishment, rejecting the life of reason and education, working on his dispensationalist charts, and creating a network of obnoxious separatist disciples. It is to Sung's great credit that he did not yield to the temptation to go down this road. In fact, he was very clear that the issue was not a personal one but one of theological health and of the very survival of evangelism.[51] Thus he had to do the best he could on

---

[49] Levi, *The Journal Once Lost*, 302.

[50] Ibid., 226.

[51] Consider the following entry in his diary. "At dinnertime, several Western clergymen inquired about

his own when he discovered that his theological education at Union rested on bankrupt theological and philosophical assumptions. He was left to proceed in an ad hoc and self-directed manner.

Sung was too well trained as a scientist to reject the treasures that were opened up by natural science. The problem with Union Liberalism was not the problem of science but the problem of ignoring the power of God. The active power of God as an agent who could act directly in the world was dogmatically excluded on principle. Sung does not address the issue directly, but it is clear that he had perceived and then encountered a transcendent Power in preaching and in his own visionary experience that could not be accounted for by natural science. This was confirmed later in his participation in exorcisms and in healings. It was even more powerfully brought home in his

---

my stay in a mental institution, and asked some questions on science and religion. They said, "Harry E. Fosdick has touched many people as well. Do you think he had been moved by the Holy Spirit too?" I answered, "I believe everything that the Bible says and only spread the story of Jesus and his crucifixion. God has given His stamp of approval upon my work, and even vindicated me. It is not for me to pass judgment on the beliefs of Fosdick; it is up to God to do so." Levi, *The Journal Once Lost*, 136.

awareness of evil and sin, together with what he saw in conversions from all sorts and conditions of wickedness. Sung never integrated this into a formal philosophical theory; but he knew implicitly that the clue to any serious resolution lay in a comprehensive vision of providence and miraculous activity both of which were governed by the power of God.

We can see the effects of this informal, ad hoc resolution of the relation between science and faith elsewhere in his life. Thus his vision of scripture focuses not on an abstract theory of scripture but in the incessant use of scripture as a means of grace. I suspect that Sung may well have been a determined fundamentalist and a hard-headed literalist in his vision of scripture (one can readily get this impression from the sources available to me), but what stands out is his use of scripture to bring folk to repentance, to awaken faith, and to nurture holiness. This signals the older pietistic conception of scripture that focuses on a soteriological reading of the text. Sung clearly holds to the reliability if not inerrancy of scripture, but this is not what holds his attention in practice. Consider how he describes his reading of scripture while locked up in Bloomingdale Hospital.

> Guided by God, I read the Bible 40 times, each time using a different scheme of study. I did not merely read every single word in the Bible, but linked the entire Bible using key words like Love, Faith and Justice and making thorough word studies. I devoured the bible as a thirsty man yearns for water. The Word provided me with the most nutritious of foods, without which I would not have been able to move forward.[52]

Sung stands here in the tradition of Wesley and early Methodism rather than with most of twentieth century Methodism. The later, in its own way, has been obsessed with the debate about authority and historical criticism. Wesley and early Methodism occupied different space. Their primary concerns are soteriological; they are in search of salvation, even though they have their own take on issues of authority and are not diffident about them.

Sung's attitude to theology is also ad hoc. He has no real knowledge of the great tradition of the church. He never mentions the Trinity. He simply works with bits and pieces of the revivalist tradition – as given him in his Methodist formation in China and Ohio – opens his bible, and reads

---

[52] Levi, *The Journal Once Lost*, 47.

it with a view to preaching the Gospel in a way that will evoke repentance, faith, and a living encounter with the power of the Holy Spirit. Even with this, the theological interpretation of his encounter with God at Union wobbles between that of the language of new birth and the language of baptism in the Holy Spirit. He is equally uninterested in articulating his vision of evangelism. From his call, he knows that he has been set apart as a herald of the Gospel, so he connects that call informally with the practices of evangelism that are already in play both in North America and China.

The Core Problems in Sung

The bottom line at this point is that Sung does not begin to deal in any comprehensive way with the intellectual crisis that Christianity faced in the West in the twentieth century. Outler at least faced it and failed, whereas Sung took the way of evasion. Thus he has left us no serious theological legacy save that worked out on his own in guest houses and hotel rooms, and he provides no resolution of the problem of faith and reason.[53] Sung

---

[53] In no way does this meant that I disparage his spiritual legacy; in reading Sung, I count myself unworthy to be in the same room.

settled for an ad hoc retrieval of the faith of the scriptures interpreted through the lens of Pentecost and informed by the residue of nineteenth century revivalist Methodism. This worked fine in the short term, but it will not work in the long-run.

Let me catalogue the problems briefly and sharply. First, the deep problem is that Sung worked as a loose cannon at the edges of the church without the resources that are essential if we are to deal with the evangelistic situation we currently face in the West. Second, Sung does not sufficiently distinguish evangelism from revival and renewal, thus there is the constant danger of treating church members as merely nominal Christians who need to be born again. In this case evangelistic preachers run the risk of being charged with the crime of assault with attempt to preach. Equally, the failure to think through the whole challenge of renewal can lead to the kind of adversarial relationship with church establishment that can all too readily banish evangelism to the margins of the church or undermine it by redefining it ways that destroys its essential practices.

Third, Sung has no interest in the place of the

sacraments in the life of faith, reducing the work of pastors to that of proclamation. Hence evangelistic practice is cut off from other pivotal practices of the faith and those who appreciate the sacramental life of the church – as we all should – come to feel that evangelism is the badge of a theological party that is liturgically impoverished.

Fourth, Sung's recipe for theology, namely, base everything on scripture, is a sure recipe for creating one more round of disillusioned fundamentalists and evangelicals, just as it was the stimulus for the failed Liberal Protestantism he detested. The same recipe will only lead to the further disintegration of the unity of the church, as we can see both in the history of Christianity in North America and currently in China and the Third World.

Fifth, Sung has no sense of the importance of the great canonical faith of the Church as represented, say, by the doctrine of the Trinity. This doctrine is no mere abstract theological speculation worked out by theologians trying to get tenure. It was hammered out specifically by local evangelists as the name of God into which Christians were baptized and was pivotal in a well-rounded vision of Christian initiation. Thus Sung yields to the temptation to move as fast as possible to the doctrine of the Christian life. He mistakenly thinks that this is all the convert needs in initiation; in reality they need much more if they are to flourish as healthy disciples.

Finally, Sung does not come near to addressing the continuing debate about the relation between faith and science. Opposition to Christianity in the name of science is now the lynch pin of the new forms of virulent atheism that are every bit as important as the debate spawned by the arrival of postmodernism. What is at issue is twofold. The background noise in our culture is either hostile or reactionary; philosophically illiterate scientists fight it out with theologically incompetent Biblicists. As a result many seekers find their commitment to science a barrier to faith. Ad hoc solutions will only take us so far at this point.

We seem now to be between a rock and a hard place. Our hands seem to be cut off from our hearts and our heads. Success in evangelism would appear to be only possible at the cost of deep Christian substance and intellectual integrity. We are caught between Chinese firecrackers and holy smoke. The only way forward is to burn through both with a Celtic tongue of fire.

3. Tongue of Fire

At The Crossroads of History

Our journey thus far has brought us to a cross-roads. We are caught between holy smoke that suffocates the church and a Chinese firecracker that threatens to burn down the church around our ears. We can capture our dilemma in terms of a set of contrasts.

One contrast centers on the visions of evangelism that will determine what we do and how we approach the challenge of evangelism. Outler saw evangelism essentially as a dimension of all that the church does. Its focus is the full formation of the faith of new disciples from beginning to end and the reorienting of all of life under the Lordship of Christ. The aim is nurturing rather than initiating life-long discipleship; any practice that fosters on-going discipleship *ipso facto* is evangelism. Sung saw evangelism as a specific ministry constituted by proclamation, invitation, and catechesis. It is intimately related to the first phases of faith; the aim is to secure new birth and initial entry into the kingdom of God. The focus of evangelism is initial commitment and primary grounding in the faith. The primary task is that of initiating into discipleship rather than sustaining discipleship.

A second stark contrast revolves around the understanding of Pentecost and its correlative implications or assumptions. For Outler, the work of the Holy Spirit in Pentecost was to enable the church to come to a fresh translation of the core of Christianity into the idiom and thought forms of the host culture. After we figure out the core, we then express it in the thought forms of the day. For Sung, Pentecost meant a fresh outpouring of the power of the Holy Spirit that brings alive the age-old Gospel of the Kingdom of God, of Christ crucified and risen from the dead. This power is signaled by effective preaching that is accompanied in radical conversion from evil, by the birth of a new life of love, by unity in the church, and by exorcism, speaking in tongues, and miraculous healing.

For Outler, Pentecost drives us to the study of history, philosophy, and the human sciences. While his work continued to deploy the language of the Trinity, it really operated within a flat, minimalist account of divine agency and action. For Sung, Pentecost drives us to repentance and a fresh entry into the kingdom of God as present in the power of the Holy Spirit made manifest in the cross of Christ. Here there is virtually no reference to the Trinity, yet this vision leans heavily not just upon providence but upon the direct, active presence of the Holy Spirit, leading to radical conversion and miraculous activity.

If we go with Outler at the height of his powers, we get a minimal and ever-changing theological package wrapped in ever-changing philosophical metaphysics and speculation (or its functional equivalent). If we go with Sung at the height of his powers, we get an exotic, supernaturalistic theological package wrapped with incisive but thoroughly ad hoc intellectual commentary. If we opt for Outler, we get high-octane intellectual energy drawn from depleting oil wells that do not connect with either the full power of the Holy Spirit or the deep faith of the Church. If we opt for Sung, we get high-octane spiritual power from the Holy Spirit drawn from wells of divinity that never run dry. These wells, however, were not successfully connected either with the full ecclesial resources the Holy Spirit gives us in the Church or with the intellectual resources we need to meet the challenges of our day.

What these contrasts represent historically is the fracturing of a rich but fragile heritage in evangelism within Methodism that existed prior to both Outler and Sung. Outler and Sung were extraordinary grandchildren of the early Methodist tradition. They were offspring of late nineteenth century Methodism, a Methodism that had already divided over slavery, holiness, the intellectual challenges of modernity, and the social gospel. For both of them Wesley was a hero, but a hero who had to be reconstructed in order to fit their vision of where we should go once the world that Wesley occupied had been shattered. They represent in reality the further fragmentation of the tradition in the twentieth century. Their competing accounts of the nature of evangelism and of Pentecost represent a parting of the ways.

The parting of the ways is visible in the relations between evangelism, the mainstream organs of the church, and the academy. To make the point sharply: the historic conception and practices of evangelism championed by Sung have become marginalized in both church and academy. Once evangelism becomes a dimension of all that we do, the alternative is dismissed as narrow and limited. Consequently, the ministry of evangelism cannot be given the specific identity and attention that it really needs if it is to be an effective part of the life of the church. In addition, evangelism in the historic sense becomes the badge of a party in the church. Evangelism gets confused with evangelicalism and vice versa.[54] Marginalization in turn means that there is not the theological and ecclesial support that is needed for healthy forms of evangelism. So evangelism becomes the property of cranks with limited theological grounding in the canonical faith of

---

[54] This was exactly the situation I encountered when I came to Perkins School of Theology to teach evangelism. Folk inside and outside the university thought that the chair in evangelism was really the chair in evangelicalism. Those who wanted to take evangelism seriously thought they had to become evangelical. There was little ability to distinguish between "evangelism," a ministry of the church, and "evangelicalism," a complex movement within classical and modern Protestantism.

the church. The result is a spiraling chain reaction in which evangelism descends initially into limbo and over time is cast into outer darkness. In the meantime, the mainstream of the church moves more and more around an academic axis that has enormous difficulty connecting to evangelism. It becomes *de rigueur* that if one is to be academic, critical, and intellectually virtuous, then (if we are lucky) only the most minimalist conception of evangelism can be tolerated. Anything substantial will be seen as inescapably tied to intellectual vice. The tension, if not split, between evangelism and scholarship becomes palpable over time.

Outler and Sung cared passionately about evangelism and about Pentecost; they were bequeathed to them as essential ingredients of Methodism with their mother's milk. So too was the quest for authentic Christian identity and genuine intellectual integrity. Yet here again we can see the parting of the ways. Outler was a highbrow scholar with a lowbrow conception of Pentecost; Sung was a lowbrow practitioner with a highbrow conception of Pentecost. Outler was a brilliant historian with limited philosophical skills who genuinely wanted to preserve the fully developed faith of the Church across the ages; regrettably he did not have the philosophical skills or resources to do so. Sung was a brilliant scientist who sought to retrieve the Gospel and the practices of the first apostles who did not have time for either serious history or philosophy; regrettably his experience at seminary drove him towards fundamentalism. Both showed true greatness in their penetrating self-criticism towards the end of their lives.

Facing the Future

The key to the future rests with finding a way to address the concerns of both Outler and Sung but without resorting to a mere method of cut and paste or by some slick geometrical image of a center drawn between two extremes. Initially we need to go back behind the fragmentation and catch a glimpse of the deeper unity that once was constitutive of evangelism within Methodism at its best. We can do so, I propose, by looking at the life and work of the great nineteenth century Irish evangelist, William Arthur. On the one hand, Arthur shared the historic Methodist vision of evangelism and Pentecost represented by Sung; on the other hand, he was totally committed to the kind of intellectual and social engagement championed by Outler.

The Ministry of William Arthur

In his day William Arthur was recognized as one of the truly great international leaders in Methodism. He was born on 3 February, 1819, in Kells, Co. Antrim, in Ireland, and died 9 March, 1901 in Cannes, France.[55] At the age of twelve the family left Kells and ended up in Newport, Co. Mayo. In his early teens he worked as a corn merchant. As a teenager, he became acquainted with the Methodists. The local Church of Ireland rector in Newport is reported to have said that William Arthur was "too wise a bird to be caught with Methodist chaff."[56] Arthur went to a service in Westport, where he was converted; there were three people present in the service, including the preacher, John Holmes. By the age of sixteen, he was preaching; thereafter, despite parental opposition, he entered the Wesleyan Methodist ministry. His father died in 1844 or 1845, possibly because of the famine; his mother immigrated to America around the same time, and died there in 1855. Early on Arthur was designated for missionary service overseas; after two years of training he set off for India

---

[55] For a very helpful biography see Norman W. Taggart, *William Arthur: First Among Methodists* (London: Epworth Press, 1993).

[56] Taggart, *William Arthur,* 3.

in 1839. He learned Kanarese, was sent to Gubbi, and went to work as an evangelist. Unfortunately he developed serious eye trouble and bad health so that, with a heavy heart, he had to come back to Britain in 1841, after only two years' service.[57]

Thereafter, Arthur's health was never good. He worked for a time in London and Boulogne; he travelled extensively as a conference speaker, and over the years wrote a spate of books. He knew and used his Greek and Hebrew, and was thoroughly fluent in French, Italian, and German. He was present in May 1848 in Paris during the revolution that ended the reign of King Louis-Philippe and led to the creation of the Second Republic (1848-52). He received an honorary A.M. degree in 1850 from Dickinson College. In 1366 he was elected President of the Wesleyan Methodist Conference, the second youngest minister to have become President. He was present at Vatican I in 1870 for the declaration of papal infallibility. While there he met with von Döllinger, the great Catholic historian and dissenter, and he wrote up the minutes of a public debate between panels of Roman Catholic and Protestant scholars on the historic relation between Peter and Rome.

---

[57] The present church building in Gubbi was opened in 1903 as a memorial to him.

For a time Arthur came back to Ireland to establish Methodist College, Belfast.[58] He never got involved in party politics as a minister, but he was deeply engaged in national debates about education and other political issues as a public commentator. He was a delegate to the General Conference of the Methodist Episcopal Church in America in 1880. He presided at two Ecumenical Methodist Conferences (in 1881 and 1892), the forerunner of the World Methodist Council. He wrote and lectured on subjects as diverse as the plight of women in India, Islam, the Vatican, Irish Home Rule, the uprising in Jamaica in 1865, the American Civil War, the emancipation of slaves, and Abraham Lincoln. He retired from active ministry in 1888, the year his wife died. For health reasons he moved to Cannes in France in 1891, where he spent the last ten years of his life. All along he worked tirelessly for the cause of missions and evangelism.

Taking Pentecost Seriously

I have already mentioned that Arthur shared Sung's conception of evangelism and Pentecost.

---

[58] This is today one of the top-tier grammar schools in Ireland. There is a building there appropriately named as Arthur Hall.

He was still embedded in a form of Methodism that saw evangelism as effectively proclamation plus initiation into the faith through the class meetings. He simply took such initiation for granted. His reflections on Pentecost also fit closely with Sung. His remarkable book, *The Tongue of Fire*,[59] which consists essentially of his reflections on Pentecost in Acts 2, became a classic in his day. It may well have been among the favorite books of Walter Rauschenbusch.[60] The book is still in print today. Let me briefly lay out Arthur's central claims and arguments.

The book as a whole is divided into four uneven parts. The first three chapters deal with the promise of a baptism of fire, the fourth with the effects which immediately followed the effects of the baptism of fire, the fifth chapter takes up the topic of the permanent effects in the church, and the last chapter rounds if off with a series of practical lessons.

---

[59] The first American edition appeared in 1856.

[60] Rauschenbusch may even have kept copies on his desk which were handed out freely to friends and acquaintances. I owe this information to conversations with Donald Dayton, but we do not have proof that this was so. Arthur shows up in Wynthrop Hudson, ed., *Walter Rauschenbusch: Selected Writings* (New York: Paulist Press, 1984).

Arthur perceptively begins by noting that Pentecost is the fulfillment of the prophecy of John the Baptist, in which John makes it clear that the ultimate purpose of the coming of Christ is to baptize with the Holy Spirit and with fire. When fulfilled, this prophecy meant that whatever Christ's personal presence and teaching had been to the original disciples, "the presence of the Spirit would be more."[61] Hence the outcome of Christ's ministry was not just the forgiveness of sins but the establishment of his kingdom within, a kingdom of righteousness, and peace, and joy in the Holy Spirit. The arrival of this kingdom was a datable event, signaled by the waiting of the disciples and Mary. Vividly aware of the once for all sacrifice of Jesus for the sins of the world and at ease with his ascension to the Father, the earthly followers of Jesus gave themselves over to fifty days of prayer in adoring anticipation of what was to come. Then the great Day arrived. There was a mighty rushing wind; there were tongues of fire resting on them; the Holy Spirit had descended upon them. They were overwhelmed with the Glory of God, they were moved to the

---

[61] William Arthur, *The Tongue of Fire: Or, the True Power of Christianity* (New York: Carlton & Porter, 1859), 15.

depths of their being, and they were baptized and immersed in the Holy Spirit, in the fire of God.

> The fire is not a shapeless flame. It is not Abram's lamp, nor the pillar of the desert, nor the coal of Isaiah, nor the enfolding flame of Ezekiel. It is a tongue; yea, cloven tongues. On each brow glows a sheet of flame, parted into many tongues. *Here was the symbol of the new dispensation.* It was a symbol of their "power:" the power whereby the new kingdom was to be built up; the power for which they had so long to tarry, and so eagerly to pray, when all other things were prepared, for which the whole world arrangement for the world's conversion was commanded to stand still.[62]

The emblems of the old era were now set aside, replaced by the emblems of water and bread and wine. The symbol of power that would energize and direct the new era was that of a tongue of fire. There was now a power

> …to stand before kings, to confound synagogues, to silence councils, to still mobs, to confront the learned, to illuminate the senseless, and to inflame the cold – the power by which, beginning at Jerusalem,

---

[62] Arthur, *Tongue of Fire*, 49-50. Emphasis added.

where the name of Jesus was a byword, she [the Church] was to proclaim His glory through all Judea, throughout Samaria, and throughout the uttermost parts of earth. The symbol is a *tongue*, the only instrument of the grandest war ever waged: a tongue – man's speech to his fellow-man, a message in human words to human faculties, from the understanding to the understanding, from the heart to the heart. A tongue of fire – man's voice, God's truth; man's speech, the Holy Spirit's inspiration; a human organ, a superhuman power: not one tongue, but cloven tongues…Blessed be the hour when that *tongue of fire* descended from the Giver of speech into a cold world! Had it never come, my mother might have led me, when a child, to see slaughter for worship, and I should have taught my little ones that stones were gods.[63]

For Arthur, then, we might say that Pentecost represented a new Day in the history of God's relations with the world, symbolized by the tongue of fire. Since the arrival of Pentecostalism, we are all aware of the hackneyed debate about whether Pentecost was constituted not by a tongue of fire

---

[63] Arthur, *Tongue of Fire,* 51-52. Emphasis as in the original.

that symbolized a radical immersion in the reality of God but by speaking in tongues. Arthur anticipated this debate. He rightly argued that tongues and miracles are by no means essential to being filled with the Holy Spirit, noting that John the Baptist was filled with the Holy Spirit from his mother's womb. Equally, miracles and tongues do not prove the fullness of the presence of the Spirit; you can have these without being filled with the Spirit. So they are neither necessary nor sufficient conditions of being filled with the Spirit. Arthur had a deeper interpretation of Pentecost. The fullness of the Holy Spirit "…declares not only that the Lord has returned to his temple in the human soul, but that he has filled the house with his glory; pervaded every chamber, every court, by his manifested presence."[64] To be filled with the Holy Spirit is for the Infinite Light of God to fill our "little chamber(s)."[65] It is to be able to do exceeding abundantly above all that we ask or think; it is to be able to abound in every good work; it is to see rivers of living water flow from within; it is to be replenished with actual virtues and practical holiness; it is to experience the dispersion of unbelief in one's soul; and

---

[64] Arthur, *Tongue of Fire*, 60-1.
[65] Ibid., 61.

85

it is to experience the witness of the Father's love and delight in adoption as children of God. In the end it is to experience a deep satisfaction at the very core of the thirsty soul. The soul now feels it has

> ... touched, yea, tasted, its supreme good, and that, for time or for eternity, it needs no more than to abide in this blessedness, and improve this fellowship. The gloomy chamber ... was entered by the sunbeams noiselessly and impalpably: no hand could feel, no ear could hear them as they came; nothing but an eye within that chamber could discern the great change. It remains the same chamber, even to the very air. So it is with the soul of man when the Lord saith, "My Father will love him, and he will come unto him, and make our abode with him." This is not only the presence of God with the spirit of man, but a special and a manifested presence.[66]

The effects of this baptism of the Holy Spirit are to be distinguished from the actual baptism itself. The effects begin with Peter's boldness and spread out to include the miracle of speaking in the languages of the thousands of pilgrims that

---

[66] Arthur, *Tongue of Fire*, 66.

filled Jerusalem for the feast. This is truly an extraordinary miracle; and it is an appropriate sign to unbelievers that confirms that God is indeed speaking through the apostles. This is an astonishing event to behold: *God is speaking* through those whose "success in preaching was conspicuously changed from talent, learning, office, or credentials, to the working of the Holy Ghost. The power ceased to be a question of natural ability, and became one of Divine gift."[67] There is here an invisible power at work. That power also shows up in the extraordinary response of the people, who, instead of mocking, now want to know what to do in response. "Never has it been recorded in other instance, that three thousand men were in an hour persuaded by one of their own nation, of obscure origin and uninfluential position, to forgo the prejudices of their youth, the favor of their people, and the religion of their fathers."[68] God was with the mouth of the apostles, and three thousand were converted in a day.

---

[67] Arthur, *Tongue of Fire*, 93-4.
[68] Ibid., 104.

Pentecost and the Success of the Church

Arthur's eloquence as he unpacks the implications of his reading of Pentecost is magnificent. He makes three points that deserve mention. First, the power of the Holy Spirit was the secret of the success of the Church in dealing with diverse cultures represented in Jerusalem on the day of Pentecost.

> On the day of Pentecost, Christianity faced the world, a new religion, and a poor one, without a history, without a priesthood, without a college, without a people, and without a patron. She had only her two sacraments and her tongue of fire. The latter was her sole instrument of aggression. All that was ancient and venerable rose up before her in solid opposition. No passions of the mob, no theories of the learned, no interests of the politic, favored her; nor did she flatter or conciliate any one of them. With her tongue of fire she assailed every existing system, and every evil habit; and by that tongue of fire she burned her way through innumerable forms of opposition. In asking what was her power, we can find no other answer than this one, "The tongue

of fire."[69]

Second, the power of the Holy Spirit was the secret of the Church's ongoing existence across the centuries.

> Religion has never, in any period, sustained itself except by the instrumentality of the tongue of fire… In many periods of the history of the Church, as this gift has waned, every natural advantage has come to replace it: more learning, more system, more calmness, more profoundness of reflection – everything, in fact, which, according to the ordinary rules of human thought, would insure to the Christian Church a greater command over the intellect of mankind, and would give her arguments in favor of holy life a more potent efficacy. Yet it has ever proved that the gain of all this, when accompanied with an abatement of the "fire," has left the Church less efficient; and her elaborate and weighty lessons have transformed few into saints, though her simple tongue of fire had continually reared up its monuments of wonder. This has been not less the case in modern times than in ancient.[70]

Third, the power of the Holy Spirit was the se-

---

[69] Arthur, *Tongue of Fire*, 110-1.
[70] Arthur, *Tongue of Fire*, 114-5.

cret of the Church's success in convincing an un-
believing world of the truth of Christianity.

> Every power has its own sphere. The stron-
> gest arm will never convince the under-
> standing, the most forcible reasoning will
> never lift a weight, the brightest sunbeam
> never pierce a plate of iron, nor the most
> powerful magnet move a plane of glass. The
> soul of man has separate regions; and that
> which merely convinces the intellect may
> leave the emotions untouched; that which
> merely operates on the emotions may leave
> the understanding unsatisfied, and that
> which affects both may yet leave the moral
> powers uninspired. The crowning power
> of the messenger of God is power over the
> moral man; power which, whether, it ap-
> proaches the soul through the avenue of the
> intellect or of the affections, *does* reach into
> the soul. The sphere of true Christian power
> is the heart – the moral man; and the result
> of its action is not to be surely distinguished
> from that of mere eloquence by instanta-
> neous emotion, but by subsequent moral
> fruit. Power which cleanses the heart, and
> produces holy living, is the power of the
> Holy Ghost. It may be through the logic of
> Wesley, or the declamation of Whitefield,

or the simple common sense of a plain ser-
vant-woman of laboring-man; but when-
ever this power is in action, it strikes deeper
into human nature than any mere reasoning
or pathos. Possibly it does not so soon bring
a tear to the eye, or throw the judgment into
a posture of acquiescence; but it raises in
the breast the thoughts of God, eternity, sin,
death, heaven, and hell: raises them, not as
mere ideas, opinions, or articles of faith, but
as the images and echoes of real things.[71]

Evangelism as Proclamation plus Formation

It is clear by now that Arthur puts much store by
proclamation in effective evangelism.[72] Yet it is
equally clear that proclamation must be soaked
in prayer and suffused with the intimate presence
and power of the Holy Spirit. This power may
also incidentally show up in the form of miraculous impressions. Miracles may have a place in
arousing interest, causing cognitive dissonance,
and confirming the truth of the Gospel. However,
"nothing is more common than for the human
mind to turn its back upon a truth, firmly believed

---

[71] Arthur, *Tongue of Fire*, 116-7.
[72] In his day the concept of evangelism was radically
underdeveloped, but we can readily see what is tacitly
in play here.

91

to be from God, deeply felt to carry eternal hopes, but demanding sacrifice of present gratifications, or of the friendship of the world."[73] Hence, if human nature is to be changed, there must be a power that gets below the surface. There must be a power that breaks through years of habit, that undercuts the deceptive lure of the world, that heals forgetfulness of God, and that overturns the relentless pull of the narcissistic ego. That power is given as the power of the Holy Spirit; without it there can be no real change in human nature. It is this power that is given at Pentecost.

Arthur is equally clear that those who come to faith must then be initiated into the church through baptism, be brought to the Lord's Table, and be knitted into a godly fellowship where the gifts of all will be called forth. They must then grow in grace through classical and prudential means of grace intentionally made available. Given that his Methodist readers would be well acquainted with this, he does not dwell upon this theme; but its presence is there for those who have eyes to see.

---

[73] Arthur, *Tongue of Fire*, 122.

The Primacy of Divine Agency

Arthur's primary concern, then, is to make sure that we acknowledge the utter primacy and indispensability of divine agency. "A religion without the Holy Ghost, though it had all the ordinances and all the doctrines of the New Testament, would certainly not be Christianity."[74] Truth, divinely adapted, is altogether necessary as an instrument in evangelism, but

> …in magnifying the instrument, never forget or bypass the agent. The Spirit in the truth, in the preacher, in the hearer; the Spirit first, the Spirit last, ought to be remembered, trusted in, exalted, and not set aside for any more captivating name. There should never be even the distant appearance of wishing to avoid avowing a belief in the supernatural, or to reduce Christianity to a system capable at all points of metaphysical analysis. If no supernatural power is expected to attend the Gospel, its promulgation is both insincere and futile.[75]

Once we recognize the importance of the agency of the Holy Spirit, it is foolish to think that

---

[74] Arthur, *Tongue of Fire*, 169. This is given special emphasis in the original.
[75] Arthur, *Tongue of Fire*, 185.

Christianity should be expected to decline with age and "grow dim before its day ends."[76]

> Our Lord's word is not, "Without Me ye can do *little*," but "Without Me ye can do *nothing*." If it then be settled that in this age, as in the first, our strength is not of nature, but of the Lord, the reasonable range of our expectation, now as then, is to be measured by his glorious power. The question no longer is, Of what are we capable in ourselves, or by ourselves? but, What can he perform? And to what extent can he manifest forth his glory by making us monuments of his power, and mirrors to display his image? The grace of his which was shed so plentifully on the believers of the first days, is not an intermittent radiance, like the flash of a human eye, but is steady as the glory which streams from the face of the sun. Waning or exhaustion it does not know; and from age to age, from generation to generation, his saints will grow more and more mature, human life will reflect the glory of the Lord, and display his power to weak mortals, beset with temptation, meet to be partakers of the inheritance of the saints in light.[77]

---

[76] Ibid., 186.
[77] Arthur, *Tongue of Fire*, 191-2. Emphasis as in the

The same sources and measure of grace are as much available today as they were to the apostles and the early church. Within the resources furnished by the Holy Spirit, miraculous gifts are auxiliaries and stand subordinate to those gifts and offices given for edification, exhortation, and comfort. As Paul instructs us, apostles, prophets, and teachers come before miracles in the list of gifts given to the Church.[78] The identification of these gifts requires attention to both call and qualifications. All of these ministries involve the Spirit-assisted ability to make known the sufferings of Christ and the glory that follows. Those who exercise these offices are to be anointed ambassadors of Christ, within or without the lineage of apostolic succession. To this end they need faith, experience, practice, and gifts. All these depend on the power of the Spirit. "If we have not the Spirit to raise up agents, we cannot preserve Christ's Church alive; if we have him, we may fully trust him to do all that is not made to depend on our own fidelity."[79]

The great danger in Arthur's day was formal propriety and intellectualism. Many ministers

original.
[78] 1 Cor. 12:28.
[79] Arthur, *Tongue of Fire*, 241.

and leaders thought that what really mattered was proper decorum and intellectual respectability. Arthur understood the place of these in the life of the church. Proper architecture and decorum do have their place; so too does the full use of the human intellect. However, these are only effective when the heart and the proclamation of the ministers of the church are infused with the fire of God. The fire of God is especially critical in times of nominal Christianity. We need the "coworking fire of the Spirit."[80] If we have failed and need to repent, we should come to God for forgiveness with confidence.

> … let us feel sure that the God of grace and mercy will hearken to our voice, will answer our prayer, will forgive our past unfaithfulness will draw near to us with new and gracious power, will enable us to go forth as giants refreshed with new wine, to bear away from the arms of adversary, in triumph and with shouting, many a lamb that is ready to be torn in pieces.[81]

In time these rescued lambs would be healed and restored to proper health, making manifest the triumph and glory of Christ "in so renewing

[80] Ibid., 287.
[81] Arthur, *Tongue of Fire*, 287-8.

the face of the earth, that the [this] image of God should be the prevalent characteristic of humanity, that peace and good-will shall take hold of nations, righteousness and truth flourish in the homes of all."[82] This was no mere fantasy. The New Testament makes clear that victory over evil was already visible in the Christian communities in Rome, Corinth, Ephesus, Colosse, and Thessalonica. The mission of the church was to "reestablish the empire of God over the hearts and lives of a race that had wandered from him, and to prepare out of the children of that race heirs meet for a pure and an immortal kingdom."[83] The very presence of this empire of the Spirit is the secret of the growth of the church, the principal lever for raising the moral standard of nations, the source of fresh agents in the ministry of the church, and the primary cause of the renewal of nominal or jaded Christians. Its presence will also mean that we have to be prepared for sudden conversions. Moreover, even though Arthur does not expect the miraculous gifts of the Spirit to appear, he insists that we should not be surprised that they do. Indeed, we have ten times more scriptural ground on which to base this expectation that for

---

[82] Ibid., 298-9.
[83] Ibid., 301.

the expectation that the fundamental blessing of Pentecost should have been withdrawn.

By this stage Arthur has run out of space for practical application. So in the final short section of *The Tongue of Fire*, he reiterates the central thesis of his work, namely, that the power of the Holy Spirit is as much available now as it was of old. The hindrances are on our end. The catalogue of hindrances as he saw it in the nineteenth century, was a lengthy one. It included neglect of prayer, unbelief, lack of faith, the lure of respectability, idle speech, party politics, sensual indulgence, the desire for literary and oratorical effect, reductionist naturalism, skepticism, nominal Christianity, the reduced versions of Christianity to be found in the churches, and a host of social sins. Against all this, however, Arthur set the promise of God to renew the earth, the large number of Christians, the readiness of God to bless afresh and bear testimony to the Gospel, and the general cultural commitment to the doctrines of Christianity. There are also many genuine witnesses to the power of the Spirit in our midst. Thus there was the real possibility of tapping into a living legacy of fire that can be handed over to a new generation. The power of the Holy Spirit is the same as it has always been. "In hope, or without hope, let us be up and doing."[84] As we are up and doing, we can pray afresh that the Holy Spirit "descend upon all the Churches, renew the Pentecost in this our age, and baptize thy people generally – [O,] baptize them yet again with tongues of fire!"[85]

Uniting Scholarship and Pentecostal Power

I have deliberately taken space to expound Arthur's vision of Pentecost because it represents a vital element in the legacy of Methodism in evangelism that was clearly picked up by John Sung. Sung's ministry was in fact driven by much the same theological vision of Pentecost as that of Arthur. In Sung the fire of the Holy Spirit burned brightly and persistently. Moreover, Arthur was clearly the harbinger of the manifestation of the miraculous signs that accompanied Sung's ministry from the beginning, including visions, tongues, and healing. We can go further when we move into the twentieth century. Arthur's vision of the work of the Holy Spirit lands him right in the middle of the Charismatic Movement, a movement that in fact pretty much adopts the theology of Pentecost laid out by Arthur with

[84] Arthur, *Tongue of Fire*, 369
[85] Ibid.,375-6.

such panache.[86]

Albert Outler was one of the truly first rate scholars who was well aware of the existence of the Charismatic Movement. Indeed it was hard for him to avoid it, for it had shown up in Dallas. Outler approached it from a distance, in a manner not unlike a curious but nervous teenager on his first date with someone who belonged to another religion. He had heard about a group of nuns at the University of Dallas who had spoken in tongues and had been cleared of canonical impropriety. Moreover, he had been assured that the speaking in tongues had been accompanied by the evident fruits of love, joy, and peace. Charismatic Christianity was clearly not his bag. Yet Outler knew the gifts and fruits of the Spirit when he saw them and was convinced that much of what he had seen was real. So he raised the intriguing question:

> What if their current charismatic renewal should prove more than a passing fad? Would they be our allies, or rivals in our commitments to a church catholic, evan-

---

[86] I take it that one of the distinguishing features of the Charismatic Movement as contrasted with Pentecostalism is that the former does not insist that tongues is essential to baptism or fullness of the Spirit.

gelical, and reformed: catholic in its human outreach, evangelical in its spiritual upreach, reformed in its constant openness to change? If nothing comes of all of this, put my comments down to a softening of the brain. But if something does come of it, don't say you weren't warned![87]

If we operate in the way Outler was hoping that developments would play out, we can say forty years later that the Catholic Charismatic Movement did not play out as he had hoped.[88] There has been no Third Great Awakening in the West; the Ecumenical Movement is now pretty much brain dead; modern mainline Protestantism is marked not by unity but vicious and expensive division. Yet we now know that we are in the midst of a world-wide Awakening of Christianity that is at long last getting the attention it deserves. We are caught in a world-wide ring of fire of the Holy Spirit and are scrambling to figure

---

[87] Albert C. Outler, *Evangelism and Theology in the Wesleyan Spirit* (Nashville, Tenn: Discipleship Resources, 1996), 54.

[88] Note I do not say that nothing good has come of the Charismatic Movement within Catholicism or elsewhere. That is a topic I cannot pursue here. My point is that Outler has not really shed the basic framework that governs his thinking.

out what to do in response.

We also now know that we United Methodists have a stake in this world-wide development, for John Sung had prepared for and predicted that world-wide Awakening as it developed in China. So the challenge of what to do with the fire of the Holy Spirit is not across the border, over there among exotic Catholics or in the dying embers of the Charismatic Movement. The challenge long ago emerged right from within the bosom of Methodism itself. Indeed, my account of Arthur shows that the fire of the Holy Spirit is absolutely constitutive of Methodism as received and developed across its first one hundred years.[89]

---

[89] This may well mean, as Donald Dayton has suggested in personal conversation, that Methodism is the most important development in Protestantism since the Reformation. This is certainly the case once we allow for the clear connections between Methodism and Pentecostalism.

Social Engagement and Canonical Doctrine

Yet we surely understand Outler's hesitations, for Outler also represents vital aspirations that are essential to Methodism, namely, the desire to uphold the deep faith of the Church in a manner that is intellectually responsible and socially engaged. We noted in our second lecture that John Sung deals with these issues halfheartedly and in an ad hoc fashion. For Outler, these matters were pivotal if we were to develop a responsible version of Christianity in the modern period. How well does Arthur fare on these counts?

Arthurs' commitment to social engagement was unquestioned. To take but one example, in his first and last books he wrote with passion and insight on the plight of women in India.[90] His commitment to the creedal faith of the Church is equally robust. In fact, he wisely wants to exploit the fact that the doctrines of Christianity are known and prized by multitudes who never knew them before. More importantly, Arthur was acutely aware of the move to deconstruct the faith in the wake of the kind of criticism we associate with the Enlightenment. He is not in the least

---

[90] William Arthur, *A Mission to Mysore* (1847) and *Women's Work in India* (1882).

complacent when it comes to the great doctrines of the faith. He worried that doctrinal betrayal was being played out in most churches:

> One would rob us of the incarnation of God, another of the Spirit of God, another of an atonement, another of providence, another of prayer; some of regenerating grace, some of ministerial unction, some of primitive fervor, some of a Lord's day; some would launch us on a sea of thought without an inspired guide; others on a moral universe without punishment for wrong; thus nearly every truth that distinguishes the system of Christianity from earthly inventions, is attacked by mining or by battery... we are sure that error is never issued into the world without doing harm; and there are strong men now doing work over which, unless other, made stronger by the might of God, undo it, generations to come will have reason to weep. For all who cannot bear to see the cross betrayed, the Holy Ghost grieved, the oracles of God degraded, the work of the Spirit in the human soul reduced to motives and emotions, and every Divine tie that connects us, as a redeemed race, with a redeeming Father, skillfully cut asunder; - for those who are not prepared to

see the Churches of England and America pass through blights such as have befallen the Churches of Switzerland, Germany, and other Protestant regions of the Continent, this is a moment when the air seems full of trumpet-notes, when every step taken on doctrinal grounds raises the echo of warning.[91]

Arthur displays here a keen sense of the importance of the great doctrines of Christianity. He has no intention of abandoning them, not least because he tacitly realized that his appeal to Pentecost already presupposed the incarnation, the resurrection of Jesus, the doctrine of the Trinity, and so on. Indeed one of the works of the Spirit is to take the great doctrines of the faith and raise them in the human breast 'not as mere ideas, opinions, or articles of faith, but as the images and echoes of real things.'

What was merely a warning in Arthur became a terrible spiritual experience in the life of John Sung. Union Seminary in the early twentieth century was a paradigm case of what happened when theologians lost their intellectual nerve and gave away the doctrinal store. We noted in Sung's case the great danger of becoming a reactionary

---

[91] Arthur, *Tongue of Fire*, 369-70.

fundamentalist who sends his brains on a holiday and ends up creating in time a situation that evokes yet one more round of bogus reconstruction of the Christian faith. Arthur was well aware of the dangers that lurk below the surface. "…alas! many who dogmatically repel error evaporate in intellectualism; others decay, under a silvered mildew of respectability; and others, professing to seek the old Christianity, content themselves with garnishing the sepulcher in which the Middle Ages buried her…"

Engaging Serious Objections to Christianity

So we rephrase our question: How did Arthur tackle the challenge of responding to the objections and criticisms that led Union into Liberal Protestantism and Sung into the foothills of fundamentalism? His strategy was simple: such issues had to be tackled head on with relevant argument and philosophical engagement. He did this in two ways. First, he put on display neglected considerations from conversion and religious experience that had to be taken seriously by anyone interested in the truth. He deployed the argument from conspicuous sanctity. "The creation of saints out of sinners is the demonstration whereby the divinity of the Gospel is most shortly and most convincingly displayed."[92] That is his neatest summary of what is at stake. Here is a more elaborate articulation.

> The miracles and prophecies of the past time are an evidence of Christianity as a system of truth; but if she be only a system of truth, and not also a power unto salvation, she adds but to the guilt of men by increasing their light, and to their misery thereafter by increasing their stripes. No miracles, no prophecies, no accumulation of arguments under heaven, can demonstrate to our neighbors at this moment that Christianity is a power which can actually make men superior to their own circumstances and their own sins; which can take men of this nineteenth century – men with sin in their blood, sin in their bones, sin in the habits, sin in the their down-sitting, sin against God, sin against their neighbor, sin against themselves, sins of self-interest and sins against self-interest, sins for happiness, and sins that wreck happiness – and out of these men, still living in the very circumstances wherein their past time has been spent, make "servants of God, free from sin, having their fruit unto holiness, and the end

---

[92] Arthur, *Tongue of Fire*, 136.

everlasting life."

The evidence of this, the only real and effective evidence, is living men who have been
regenerated, and whose good works plainly
declare them to be of our Father who is in
heaven. We, too can say, that "God has sent
his Son Jesus to bless" our neighbors, "in
turning away every one of them from his
iniquities;" but how unimpressive would be
our saying it, were there none to whom we
could point them, and add, "These are our
epistles, known and read to all men!"[93]

---

[93] Arthur, *Tongue of Fire*, 302. Technically the argument deployed by Arthur is a form of the argument
to the best explanation. This is clearly brought out in
the following passage. "When conversions are very
numerous, in proportion to the human instruments,
the agency of God is much more strikingly manifested
than when they are few. Although the man who, by his
own experience, knows what it is to pass from darkness to light, will see an evidence of the power of the
Holy Ghost in any and every true conversion; those
who have no such experience, easily avoid concluding
that a supernatural power is in action, so long as they
can trace an imagined proportion between the agency
and the results. If a few people are turned from their
sins by many preachers, it seems no more than natural
if a few holy men are found in a multitude, it is only
another proof, they think, of the fact that there will be
a certain number of good people among the wicked.

Second, Arthur sought to rebut the standard arguments of positivism, agnosticism, and deism, as he found them in his own times. This was no mere casual exercise on his part. In the case of the positivism of Auguste Comte, he followed Comte's intellectual journey carefully and read him in the French original. In all Arthur devoted no less than four major publications to this work, including two books.[94] I cannot go into a serious evaluation of these arguments here. Suffice it to say three things. First, Arthur's contribution is not among the first rank of philosophical discussion, but they are an amazing achievement when read as the work of an amateur intellectual seeking to

---

But if a large number of thoughtless youths, or confirmed sinners, become devoted to God through the instrumentality of some one preacher, and if this extends to neighborhood after neighborhood, a feeling falls upon spectators that *it is not be accounted for by reasoning about proportion, but by the operation of a superior power.*" See ibid., 312-3. Emphasis added.

[94] *Difference between Physical and Moral Law* (1883), *Religion without God* and *God without Religion* (published initially in parts from 1885), and *On Time and Space, Two Witnesses of a Creator* (1887). For a review of these materials see Taggart, *William Arthur,* chap. 8. Taggart underestimates the weight of Arthur's argument and their continued relevance to our current situation.

meet the objections of his day. Second, while the material is dated, many of his insights and arguments are still profoundly relevant in our day. Third, this work makes it abundantly clear that Arthur displays conspicuous intellectual responsibility in tackling the criticisms and objections to the Christian faith that inevitably crop up in evangelism.

Celtic Wit and Fire

It is time to bring these lectures to a conclusion. By looking at the contributions of three great figures in Methodism I trust that I have convinced you that we have inherited a remarkable legacy. We were born in an amazing outburst of evangelistic activity; our initial success in evangelism was no accident. Evangelism was built into the very fabric of our identity. While we did not develop an explicit theory and practice of evangelism, it is not difficult to make explicit the tacit components in play. Our goal in evangelism was clearly directed to reaching those who did not know God and aimed at making real Christians. Hence we aimed at effective initiation into the kingdom of God. Our practices were constituted by proclamation and effective follow up. We did this work from within the bosom of the Church, tacitly relying on the scriptures and the great doctrines of the faith. We also sought to do this work in a manner that connected to the culture without surrendering the Gospel or the classical faith of the Church. This required extensive intellectual work in dealing with both popular and sophisticated objections to Christianity. We were committed to both revelation and reason. Above all, we rediscovered the critical place of the Holy Spirit in the work of evangelism. To put it simply, we were from the beginning driven by Pentecost. All of these elements are embodied in the life and work of William Arthur.

For a host of reasons this relatively coherent network of theory and practice collapsed and the tradition of evangelism fragmented. The fragmentation shows up dramatically in the life and work of John Sung. Sung kept alive the conception of evangelism that saw it essentially as proclamation plus catechesis. He also experienced dimensions of Pentecost that have now blossomed into a world-wide Awakening inside and outside of his native China. Given his dramatic experience at Union Seminary, it is not in the least surprising that he had little interest in social engagement or in dealing with the aftermath of the Enlightenment. Frankly, his western theological education turned out to be disastrous. In a way, this did not matter, for Sung had a special call of God on his life that was utterly unique.

The fragmentation shows up in a very different way in the ruminations of Albert Outler on evangelism. Outler reconfigures evangelism not as a specific ministry of the church that focuses on Christian initiation but more as a dimension of all that the church does to express Christian life and witness from the cradle to the grave. Evangelism is really directed towards nurture rather than initiation. Hence the conception and practice of evangelism he inherited collapsed. Evangelism was relegated to the margins of the church, or it was reworked so that it became pretty much everything and anything we do in the church. The fundamental strategy for dealing with the objections to Christianity also changed. Retreating into some kind of evangelical or fundamentalist backwater was out of the question. So Outler looked to historical investigation to enable him to discern the unchanging core of Christianity and then sought to translate that core into the intellectual structures of his day. This was an essentially destabilizing strategy which has led to further fragmentation as it has played out in United Methodism under his tutelage. In my judgment this is a significant cause, but not the only cause, of our decline. If we continue on this course, the decline and death of United Methodism as a serious agent in evangelism is inevitable. Those parts of United Methodism that avoid these mistakes, will, I predict recover and flourish.

It is clear to all serious observers that we cannot continue as we have done over the last generation. There are no quick fixes at this stage. However, I have no doubt that the heart of our dilemma and of any serious hope for the future lies in a new Pentecost in United Methodism.

These lectures make it clear, however, that we cannot resort to the Holy Spirit as a cheap labor-saving device. Proper appropriation of the work of the Holy Spirit cannot be done in a vacuum. The Holy Spirit comes laden with a host of gifts, and we all have our own ways of cherry-picking the work of the Spirit since Pentecost. To fully appropriate the gifts of the Spirit we will need, for example, to take with radical seriousness the full canonical heritage of the Church. This in fact is the theological core of the faith that Outler sought with such energy, but that turned into a will of the wisp in his hands in the 1960s and 70s. We will also need to tackle the serious objections to the

113

Christian faith that abound in our culture, and do so in a way that is really intellectually rigorous. The strategy of translation is a failed strategy. We have in fact extraordinary resources available to us today to deal with the current objections to the Christian faith that were not available to Outler. Regrettably these resources are simply unknown in elite United Methodist circles; we are still captivated by superficial conceptions of relevance and theological reconstruction that ultimately destroy the faith from within. I assume, of course, that we will also need to continue our commitment to realistic and effective social engagement, for the Gospel and the faith of the Church have public dimensions that cannot be abandoned.

What we need above all is the fire of Pentecost in our midst, a fire that reignites the Celtic tongue of fire that first brought Methodism to America from Ireland over two hundred years ago. I am frankly skeptical that United Methodism as a church – as a corporate body – will take this seriously, much less explore in any detail what this might mean in practice. We are still too addicted to the failed practices of the recent past to opt for radical change. We are too preoccupied with sex and global realignment, we are too fragmented, and we are too scared of Chinese fireworks to make the changes that are necessary. We are still living in holy smoke.

My aim in these lectures has been modest. I have not spelled out the changes I would love to see in United Methodism in evangelism. To do so would be premature and unpersuasive until we sort out the legacy we have inherited. I want to leave a record of what we once were – of what the fire of the Holy Spirit once accomplished through us – and of what the fire of the Holy Spirit is now doing across the globe. Our world is in fact surrounded by a Ring of Fire. I would dearly love to see United Methodism as a church fall headlong into that Ring of Fire. Happily, there is nothing to stop you and me from falling into that Ring of Fire. I leave the last word to Albert Outler. "If nothing comes of all of this, put my comments down to a softening of the brain. But if something does come of it, don't say you weren't warned!"

About the Author

Born in Northern Ireland in 1947, William J. Abraham currently teaches at Perkins School of Theology, Southern Methodist University in Dallas, Texas. Educated at Portora Royal School, Enniskillen and Queen's University, Belfast, Abraham went on to receive a Master of Divinity Degree from Asbury Theological Seminary in Wilmore, Kentucky, and a doctorate in Philosophy of Religion from the University of Oxford, England. In 2008 he was awarded the D.D (h.c.) from Asbury Theological Seminary.

Other books related to this volume that he has published include: *The Coming Great Revival: Recovering the Full Evangelical Tradition* (Harper and Row, 1984), *The Logic of Evangelism* (Eerdmans, 1989), *Waking from Doctrinal Amnesia* (Abingdon, 1995), *The Logic of Renewal* (Eerdmans, 2004), *John Wesley for Armchair Theologians* (Westminster/John Knox, 2005), *Aldersgate and Athens* (Baylor University Press, 2010), and with James E. Kirby, *The Oxford Handbook of Methodist Studies* (Oxford University Press, 2010).

Professor Abraham is the Founder and President of Oasis International Missions (www.oasisxm.org) which works with indigenous churches in Kazakhstan, Nepal, and Romania. He has accepted invitations as lecturer and preacher throughout the United States, and in Great Britain, Ireland, Malaysia, Singapore, Central Asia, Costa Rica, New Zealand and Australia.

www.ingramcontent.com/pod-product-compliance
Lightning Source LLC
LaVergne TN
LVHW021513080426
835509LV00018B/2504